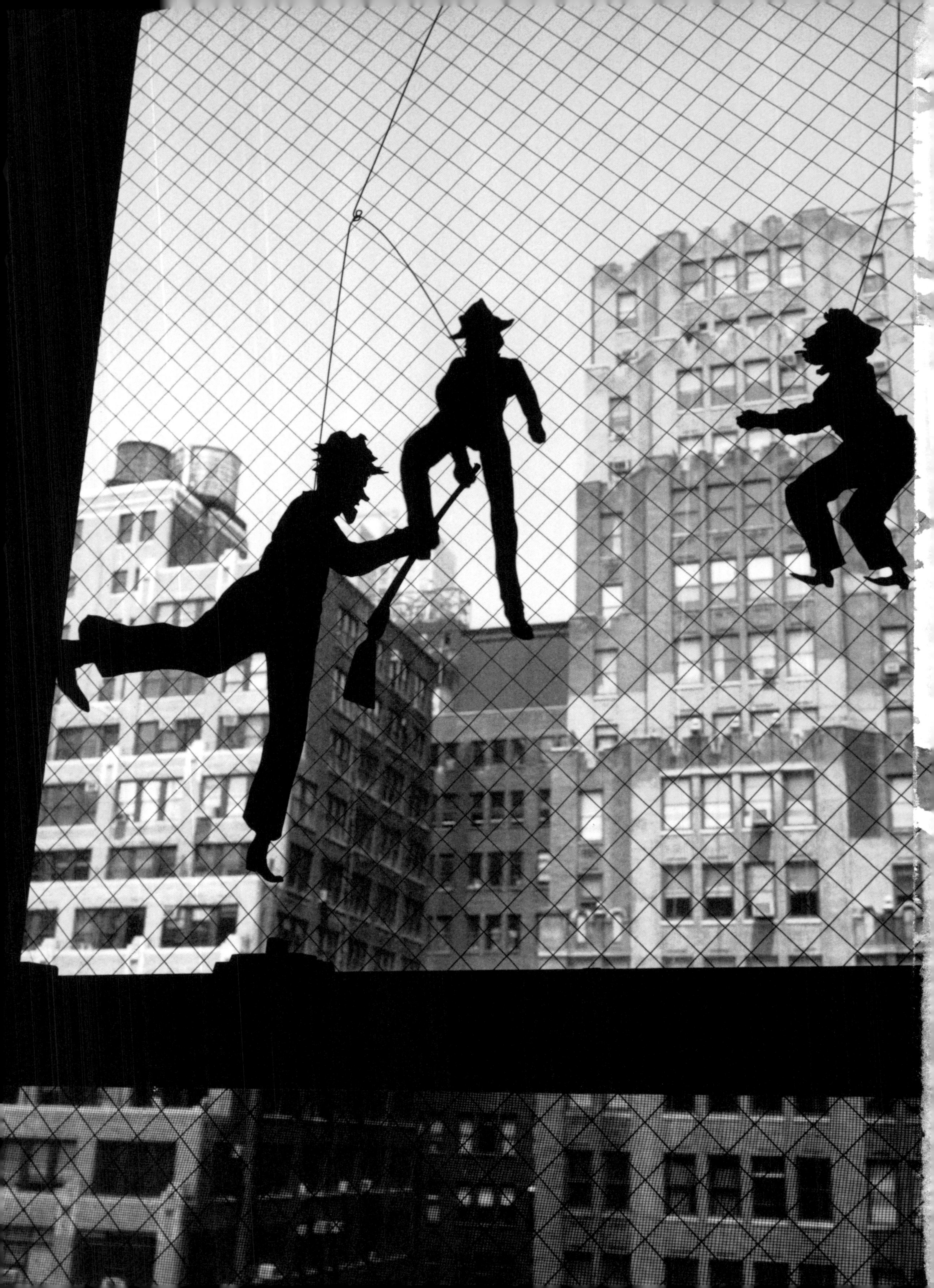

demons, yarns & tales
TAPESTRIES BY CONTEMPORARY ARTISTS

foreword by Christopher Sharp

introduction by Sarah Kent

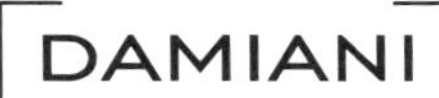

DAMIANI

in association with

BANNERS OF PERSUASION

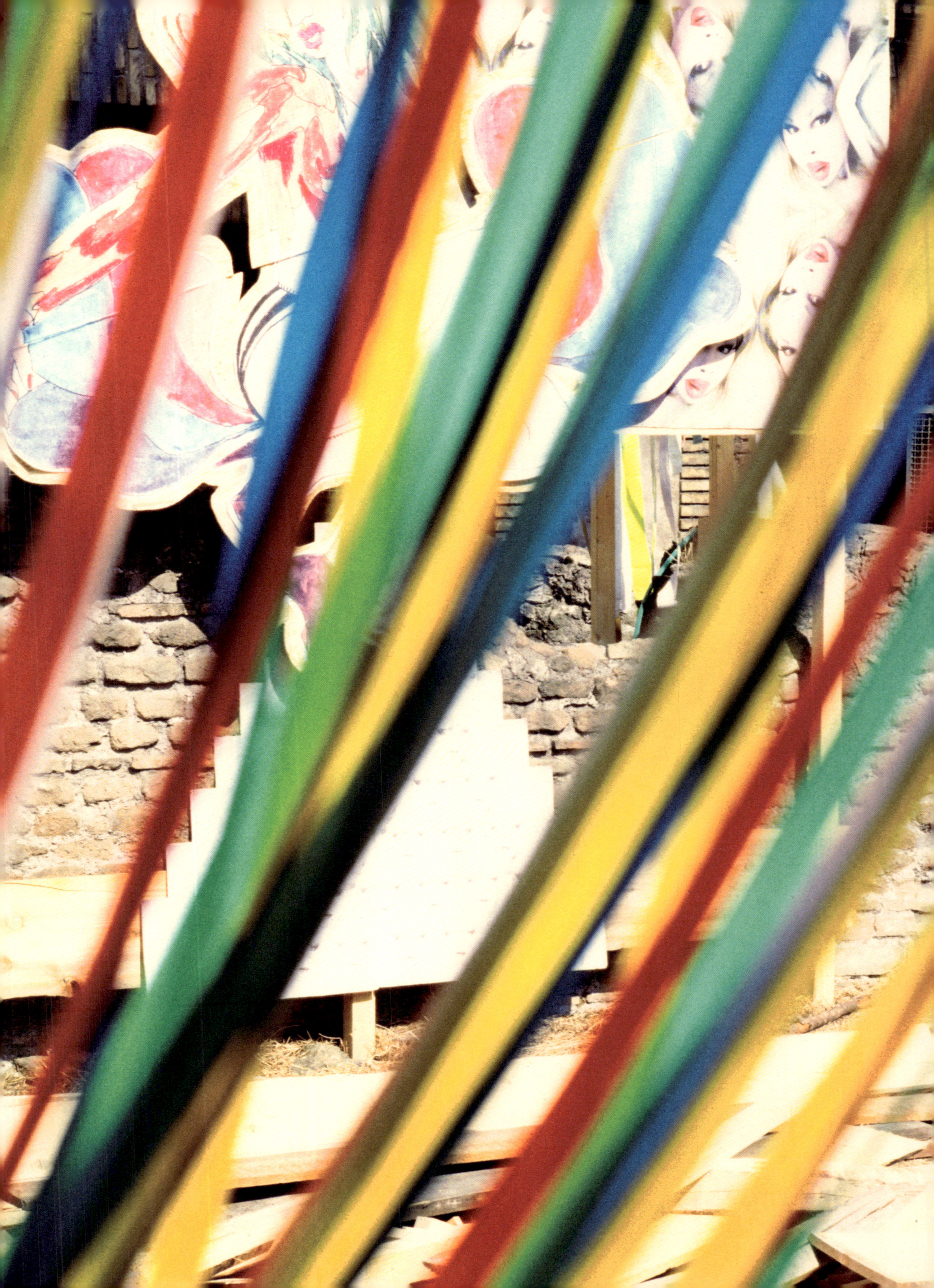

Contents

foreword

Christopher Sharp

When we invited a group of internationally renowned artists to explore a medium foreign to their usual practice, we were asking them to take a voyage into the unknown, leaving their area of comfort to work in unfamiliar territory. The medium was that of tapestry; a lost art made redundant by the sheer expense of its production and non-compliance within a world impatient to conform to the ease of mass-production in an era of convenience. The art of tapestry and the knowledge of its craft faded long ago in much the same way as the magnificent tapestries themselves disintegrated.

The exhibition is an experiment within this lost world and addresses themes of translation and transformation. The works pose visual and tactile questions concerning the translation of meaning. Three years in the making, the exhibition reveals the shifting transformation of each artist's unique visual style from his or her known medium into the uncharted and the unknown. Initially one is preoccupied with technical matters: unfamiliar colours, the texture of the material, the properties of the different threads and the complexity of the weave. Then, as the work develops, the new medium begins to contribute to, rather than compromise, the finished work; giving birth to a thoroughly contemporary art form, evolving naturally from its historical past. The handwoven setting proves itself to be an alternative soft canvas; warm, tactile, able to represent ideas and images on a vast scale, both in terms of imagination and physical presence.

The notion of tapestry, an art form with a complex and well-documented past, is thereby transformed, enabling us to reconsider it as an illuminating and revelatory format for today's world.

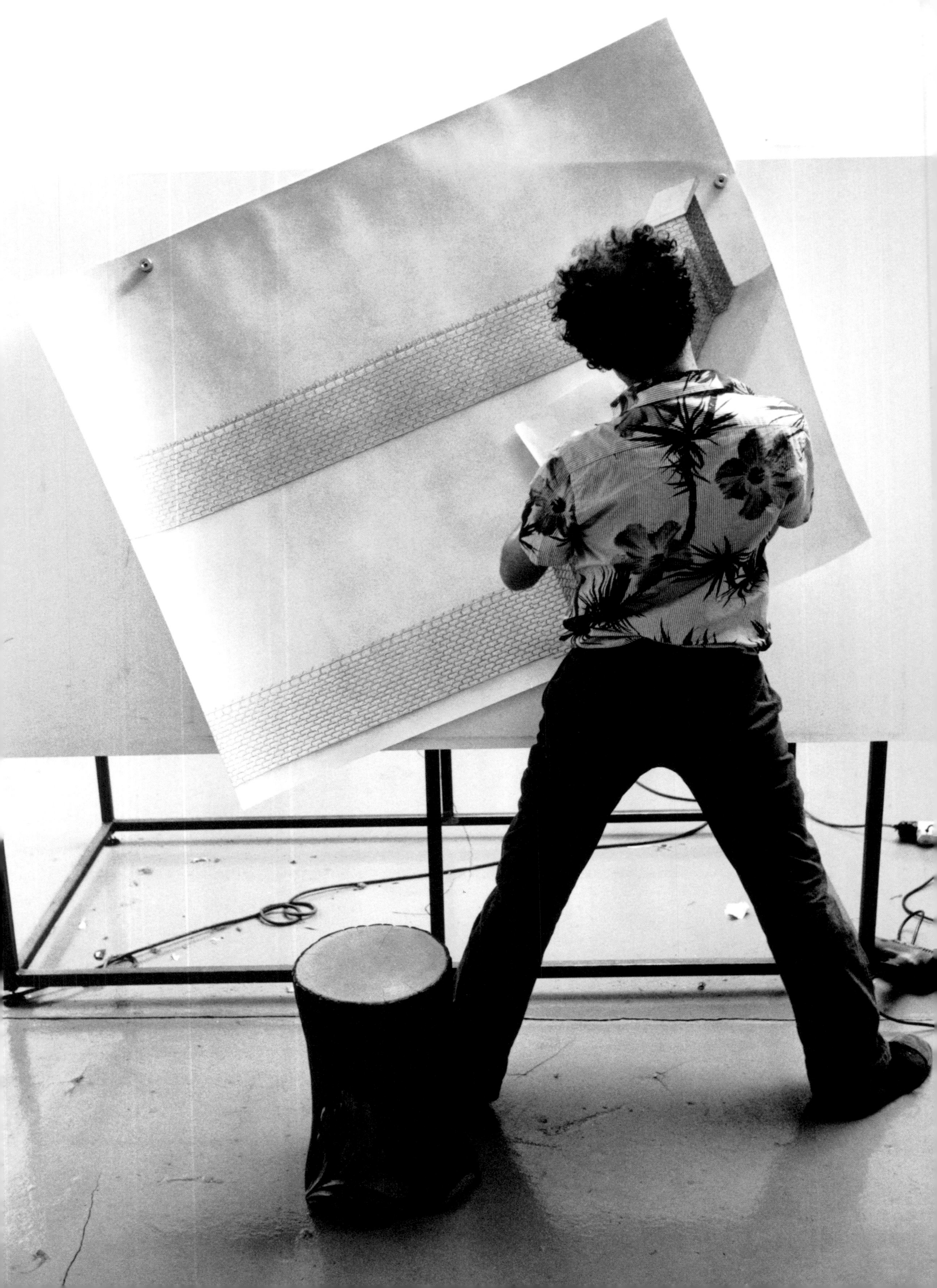

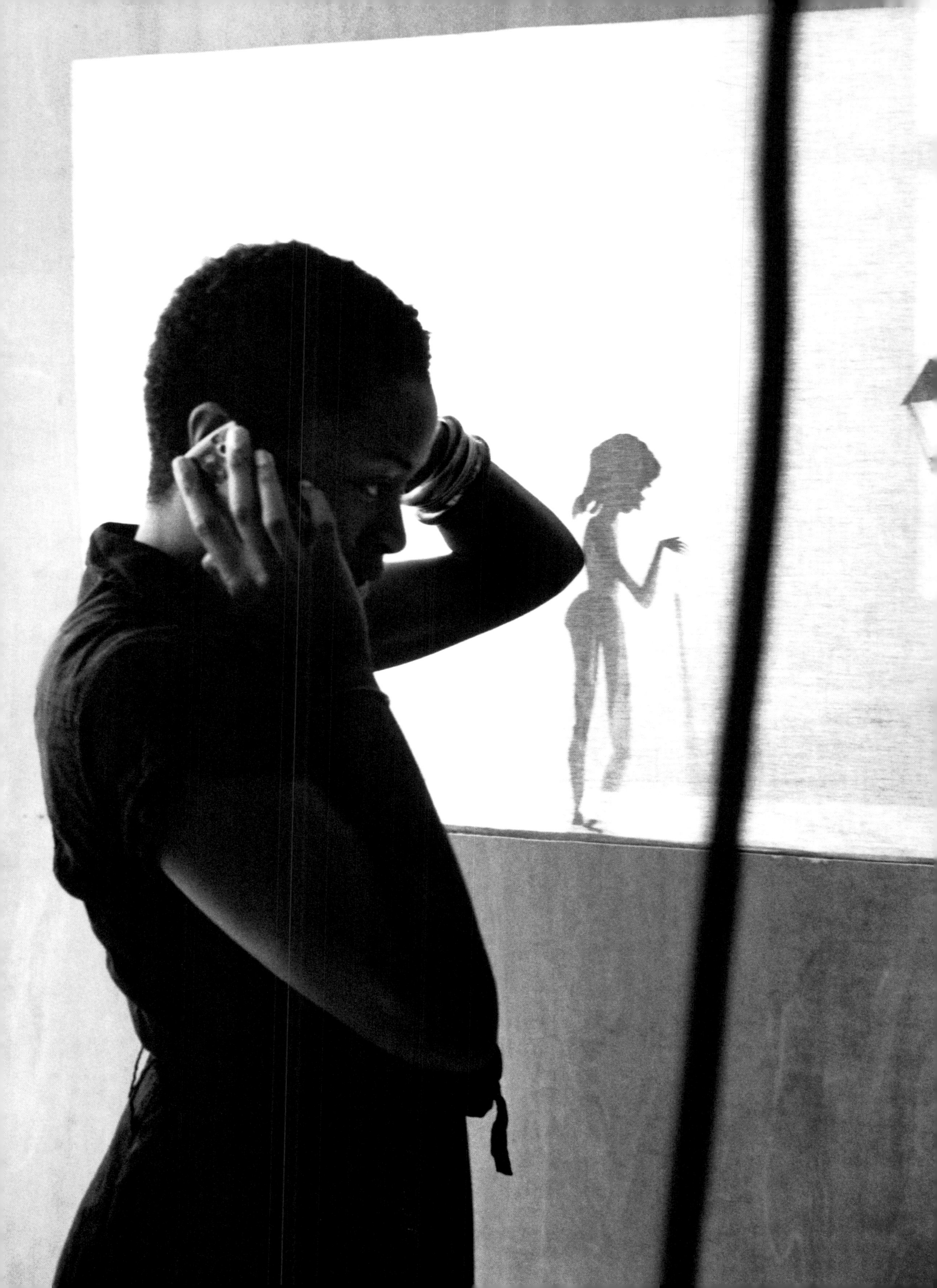

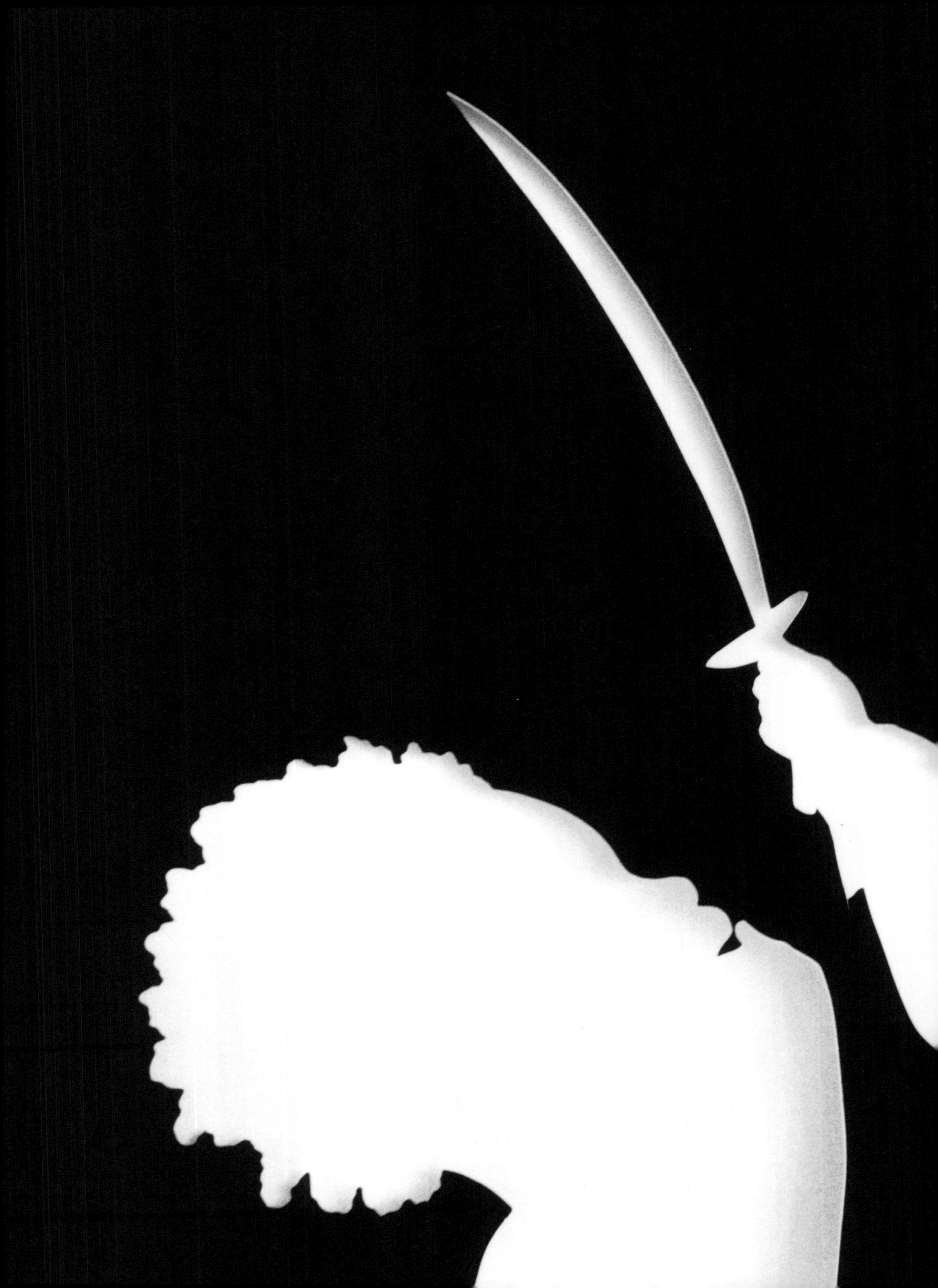

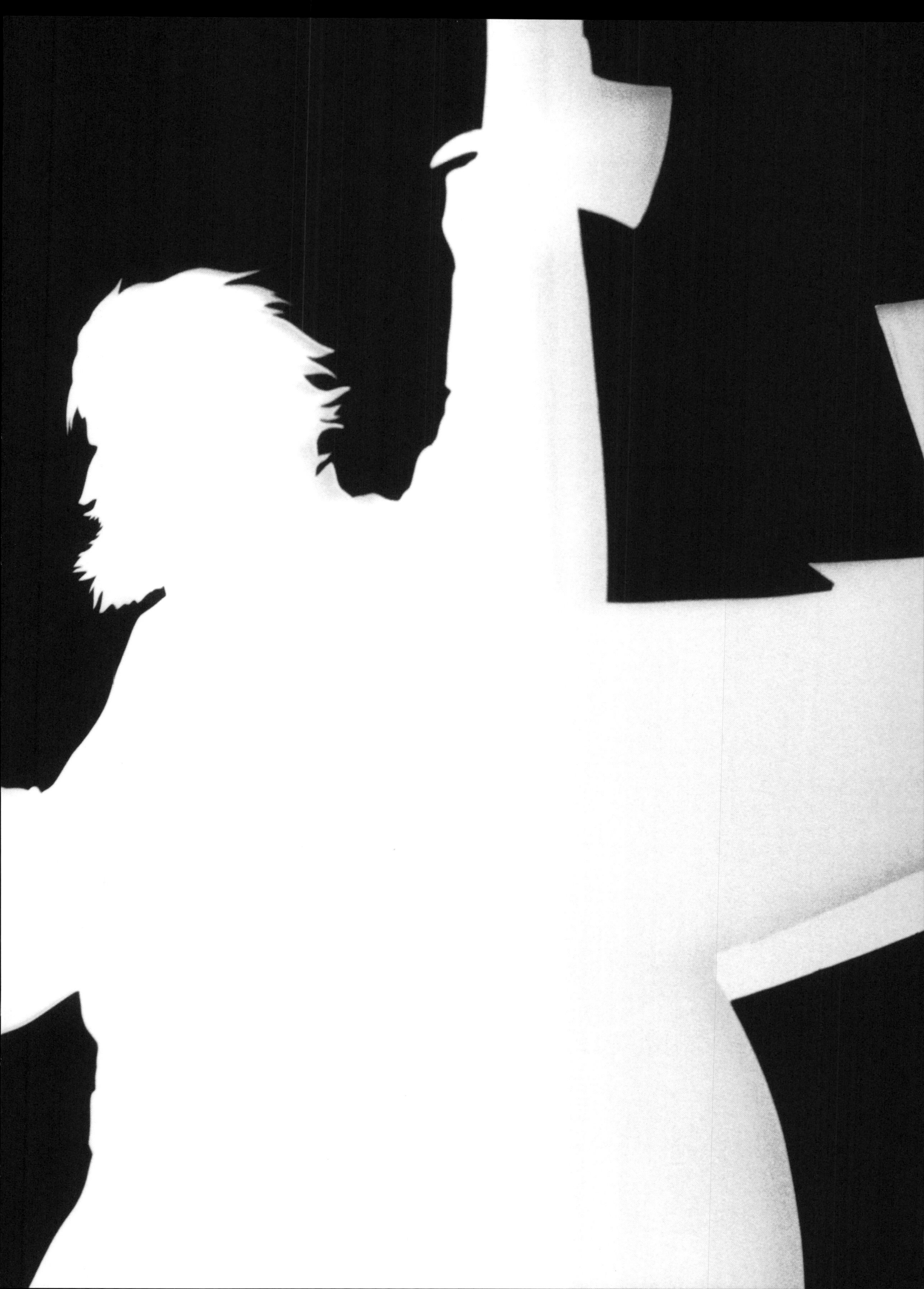

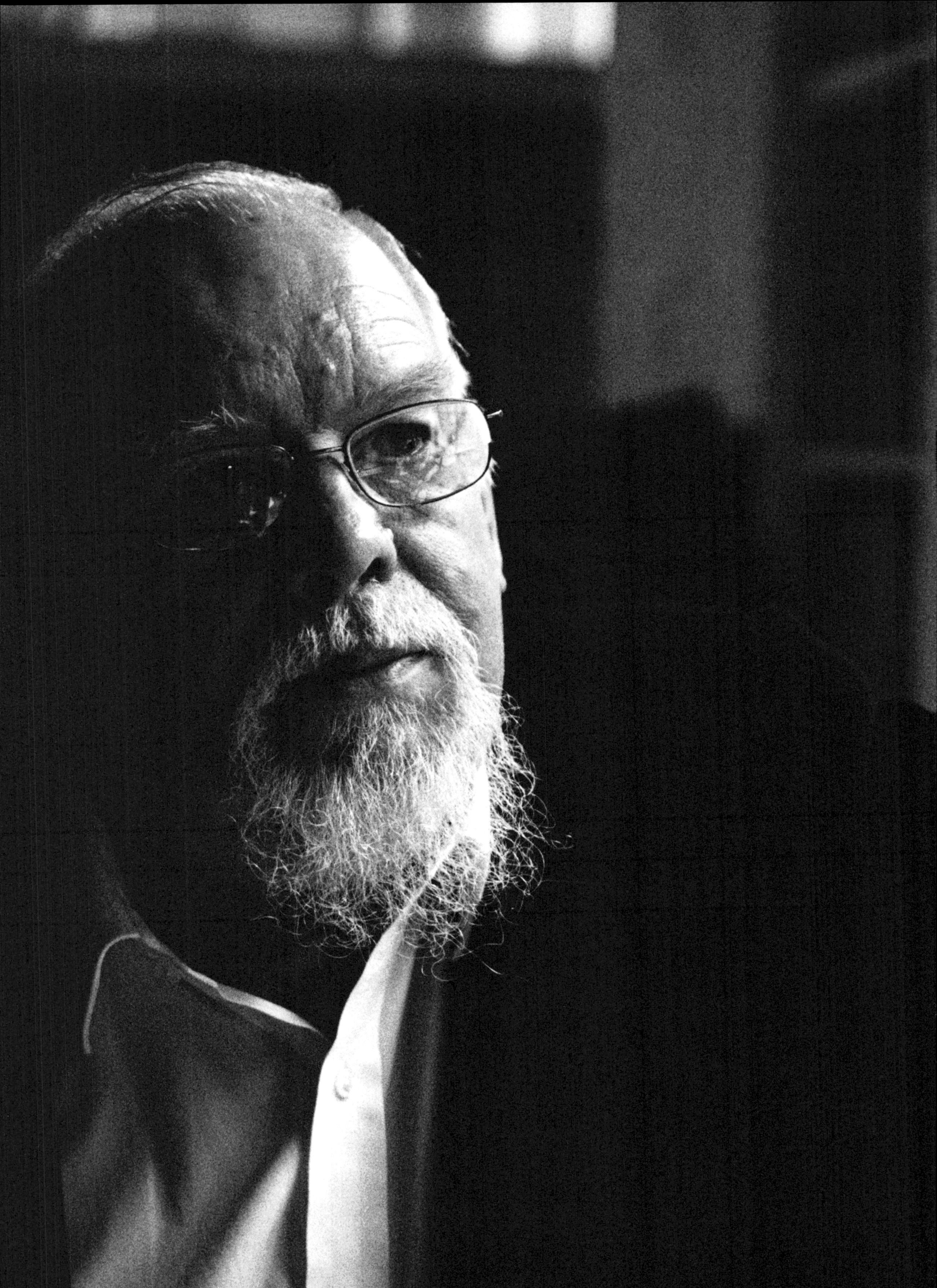

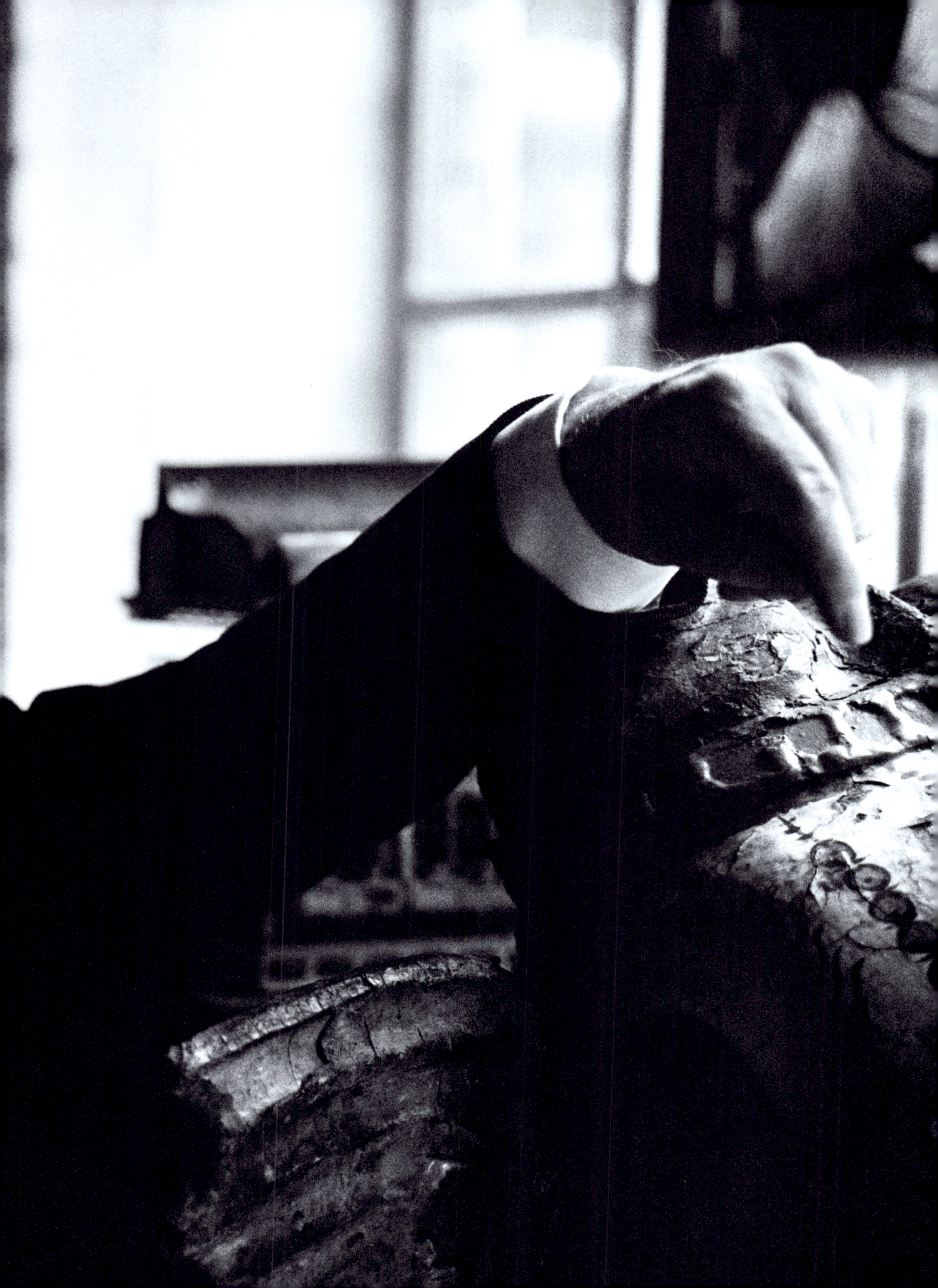

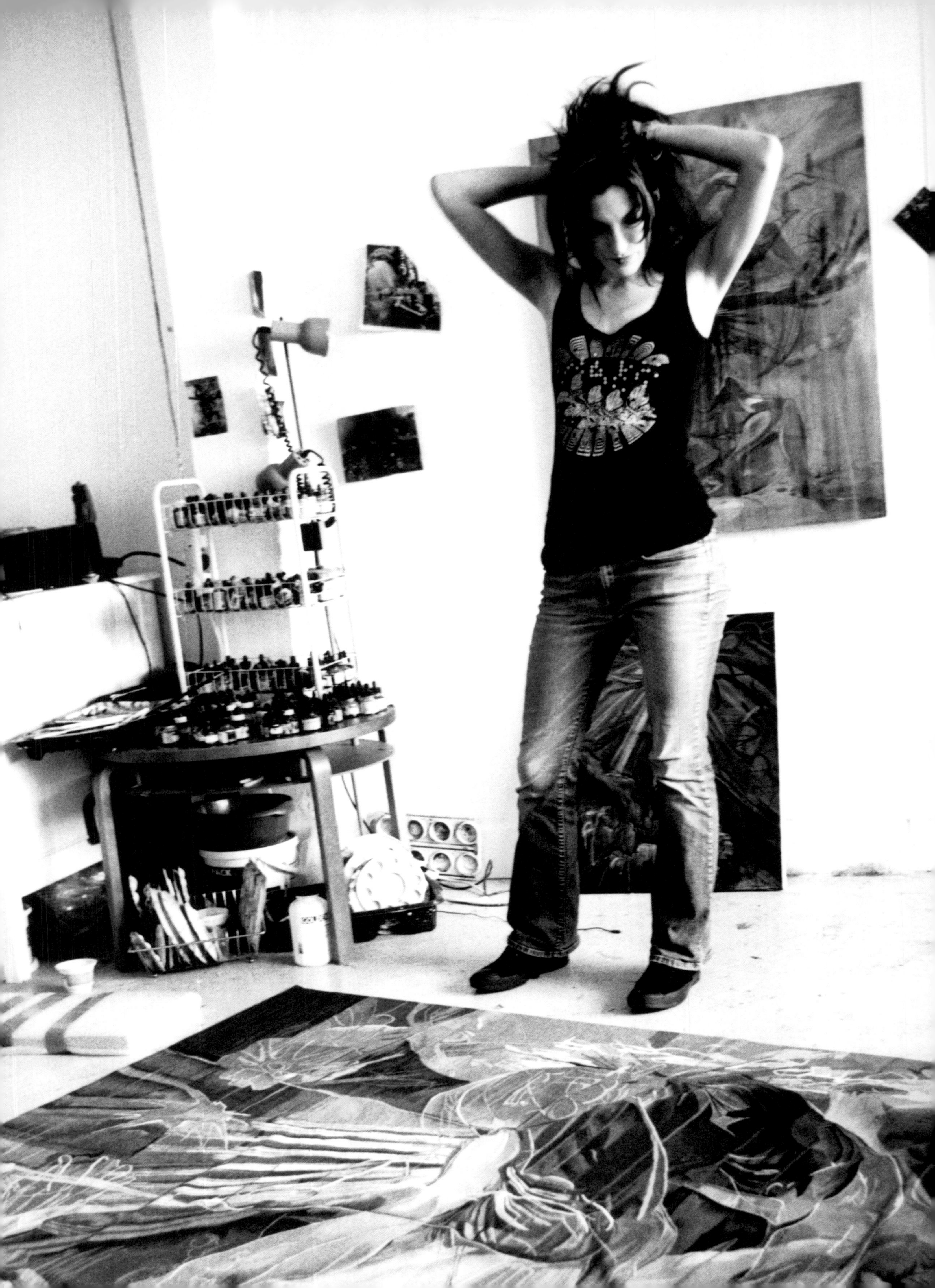

introduction

Sarah Kent

To be perfectly honest, I've never been much interested in tapestries; many have faded to monochrome echoes of their former glory, and this makes them hard to appreciate. Then there are the subjects – battles, treaties, hunting scenes and Biblical stories – which seem absurdly overblown in relation to the modesty of a medium which, despite its historical links with royalty and the aristocracy, has always struck me as essentially domestic. The simple truth is that I prefer paintings, and most other media. I'm a typical example, in other words, of pure prejudice.

Yet something about this project appealed to me. Of the fourteen artists taking part, most have no previous experience of designing a tapestry; nor is their work particularly well suited to the medium. I could easily imagine Beatriz Milhazes adapting her highly decorative abstractions for a woven design; yet her tapestry is a real surprise, because it is far more subdued in colour and shape than her paintings. How, though, would a maverick like Gavin Turk, who usually works in three dimensions, respond to such a challenge? His intriguing map of the world is the kind of oddball response that makes this project such a success. I was surprised to discover that many of the artists already had an interest in tapestry prior to their involvement in the project. Gary Hume, avaf and Julie Verhoeven, for instance, all mentioned their love of an exquisite group of mediaeval tapestries called 'The Lady and the Unicorn'.[1]

The artists invited to take part come from London, New York, Caracas, Rio de Janeiro and Paris; some know one another, but most do not. Their ages range from to 29 to 76 and their work differs dramatically from paintings (Ghada Amer & Reza Farkhondeh, Peter Blake, Gary Hume, Francesca Lowe, Beatriz Milhazes and Shahzia Sikander), to assemblages (Fred Tomaselli), sculptures and installations (avaf, Gavin Turk, Kara Walker), ceramics (Grayson Perry), prints, drawings and illustrations (Paul Noble, Peter Blake, Julie Verhoeven) and videos (avaf). It's obvious from this list that no house style prevails;

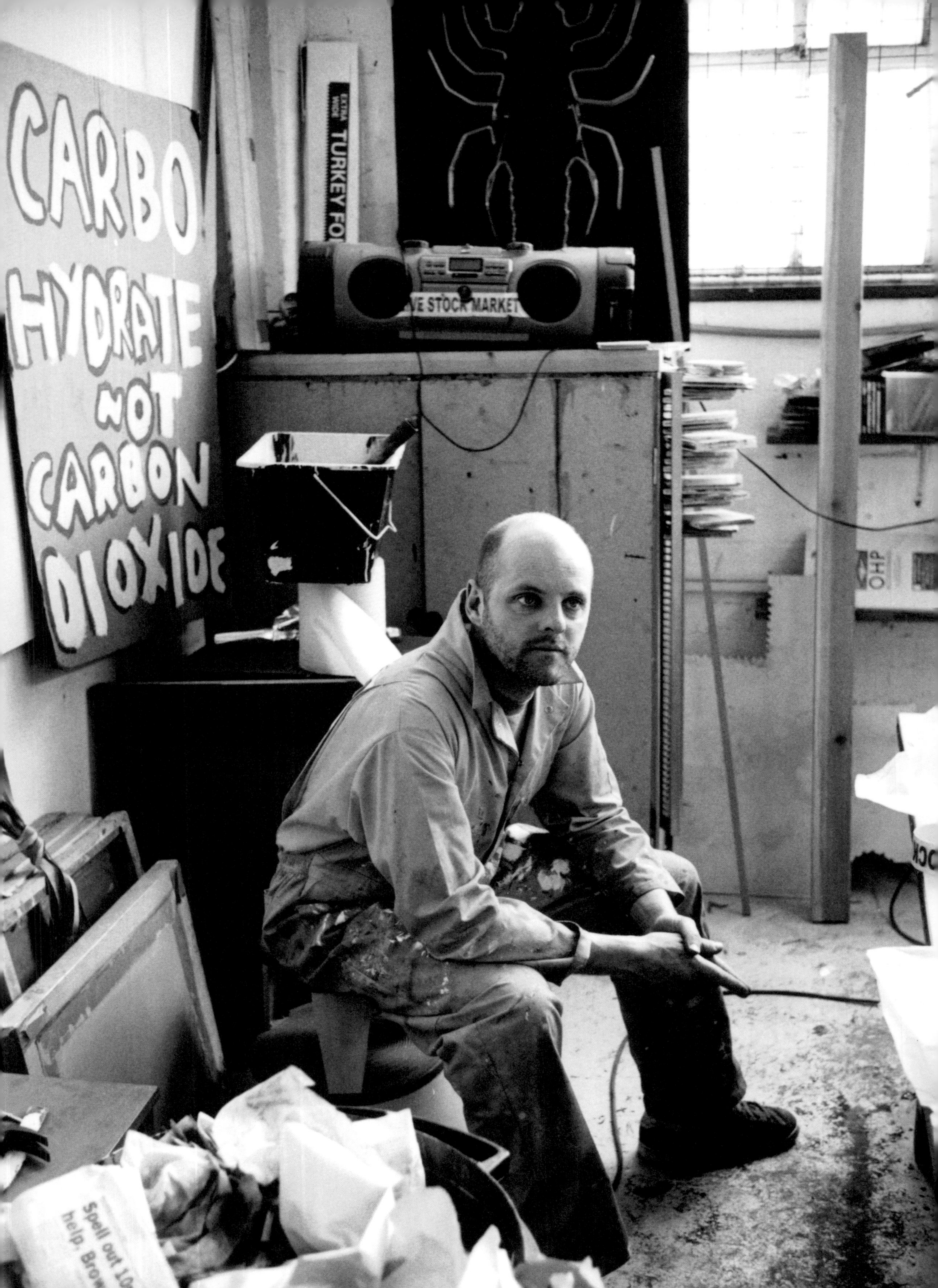
CARBO
HYDRATE
NOT
CARBON
DIOXIDE
TURKEY FO
STOCK MARKET
OHP

even among the painters, the work ranges from jazzy, hard-edged abstraction, to gauzy figuration and pop art.

I decided to speak to all the artists. I was curious to know how they set about making a design for a medium they had so little experience of, and if they felt their involvement in the project had been worthwhile. At the time of writing, some of the tapestries are still being made. When I talked to them, Gavin Turk, Ghada Amer and Kara Walker were waiting anxiously to find out how well their ideas would be translated, but everyone who'd seen their tapestries expressed delight at the quality of the finished product.

Ultimately, this is what made me want to write the catalogue. I was astonished by the perfection and beauty of the tapestries and overwhelmed by their fidelity to the original artwork or, where mimicry was impossible, by their inspired interpretation of the source material. This process of translation requires enormous skill. From the original artwork, a full-scale weaver's graph has to be produced containing an outline drawing of the design, annotated with precise colour references for the weavers to follow. What a task!

With its infinitesimal variations on the colour grey, Paul Noble's minutely detailed drawing must have presented an almost impossible challenge. Then there's the problem of how to achieve diagonals and curves; because a tapestry is made from interlocking vertical and horizontal threads, it is virtually impossible to create curving or diagonal lines that don't have a stepped profile. With its fleet of triangular shapes aligned on the diagonal, Jaime Gili's painting could have been made for the express purpose of testing the weavers' ingenuity. And with her web of interlocking arcs and circles, Beatriz Milhazes must have created similarly intractable problems. Yet in each case, the weavers have managed to produce clean, sharp outlines that, to the naked eye, appear absolutely fluent – not a zig-zag in sight! The weaving house making the tapestries is in China, where

this is not a traditional craft. The company was set up only ten years ago and employs the Flemish weaving techniques used by the famous tapestry makers of Aubusson. It takes a long time to produce each tapestry partly because of the intricacy of the work, but also because the factory is situated in a rural community north of Shanghai and the weavers, all of whom are women, work part time so they can be free to help in the fields and gather in the harvest.

The inspiration for the project came from Christopher and Suzanne Sharp; they felt it was time to broaden their remit from rug design and chose tapestry because of its links with painting – because both canvases and tapestries hang on the wall and because, throughout the long history of the medium, artists have played a crucial role in making designs for tapestries. In the twentieth century, a revival of interest encouraged major figures such as Picasso, Matisse, Léger, Kandinsky, Braque, Ernst, Moore and Vasarely to produce tapestry designs and, in recent years, artists as diverse as Chuck Close, Craigie Horsfield and William Kentridge have undertaken large-scale tapestry projects. The medium, it seems, is here to stay. And, if the quality of these fourteen tapestries is anything to go by, it will continue to flourish.

[1] The mediaeval cycle known as 'The Lady and The Unicorn' consists of six tapestries respectively titled 'Love', 'Hearing', 'Sight', 'Touch', 'Smell' and 'Taste'. Featuring a lady, lion and unicorn in an exquisite formal garden, they are in the collection of the National Museum of the Middle Ages, Paris.

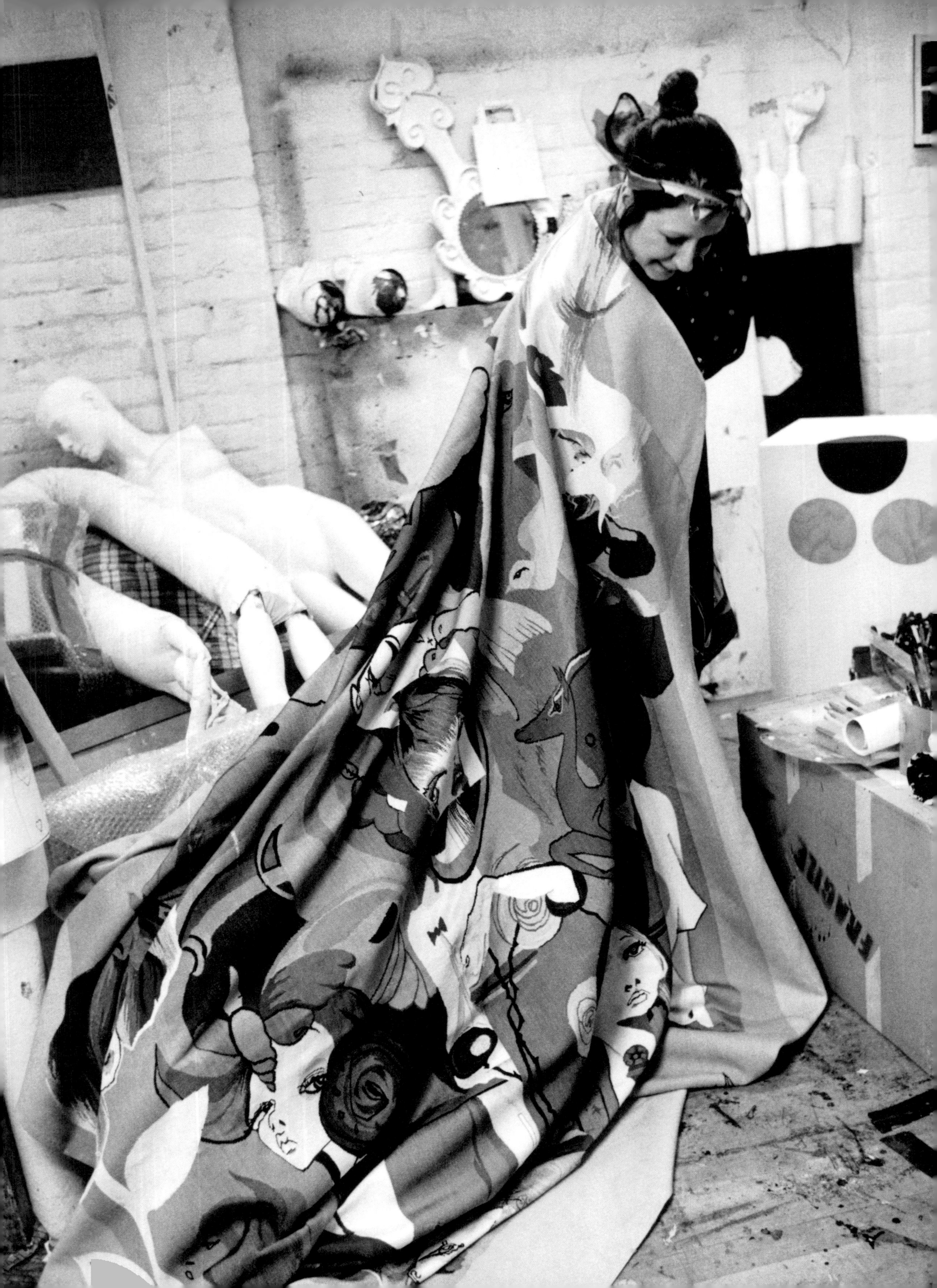

the tapestries

A Warm Summer Evening in 1863
Kara Walker

Kara Walker is best known for confrontational wall pieces
featuring people cut out of black paper. Cutting paper
silhouettes became a fashionable pastime for ladies in
the eighteenth and nineteeth centuries. Walker uses
this outmoded craft to portray a cast of stereotypical
characters from the Deep South, in the days when
slavery dictated everyone's place in the social hierarchy.
Southern belles, top-hatted gents, pickaninnies,
black mammies and uncle toms interact, sometimes
coquettishly; more often, though, they engage in
murderous acts involving extreme violence and cruelty.
'The history of America is built on this inequality, this
foundation of racial and social inequality', Walker has
said. 'And we buy into it. I mean whiteness is just as
artificial a construct as blackness... and my project
is about trying to examine what it is to be an African
American artist, so it's not just an examination of race
relations in America, today... it's about how do you
represent your world, given what you've been given?'[1]

In 2005 she made a series of prints based on illustrations
from 'Harper's Pictorial History of the Civil War', a
book published in 1866 which has long been a source
of inspiration. Over each print she silkscreened the
silhouette of a black figure whose presence seems to
contradict the scene beneath. This throws into doubt
the version of history portrayed in the illustration while
pointing out the absence of African-American voices
from the records.

Innocently titled 'A Warm Summer Evening in 1863',
her tapestry is based on an engraving first published in
a newspaper; it shows rioters burning and looting an
orphanage for coloured children in New York. As the
flames take hold, black children flee the building only
to be met by an angry mob. The quality of the tapestry
is amazing; every flicker of fire and puff of smoke is
translated in perfect detail along with the crude marks
made by the engraving tool. As in the print series, the
scene will be partially hidden by the silhouette of a
hanged woman – the victim of a lynching. 'The figure will

A Warm Summer Evening in 1863
1.75 x 2.5m (5ft 9in x 8ft 2in)
Wool tapestry and hand cut felt silhouette figure, 2008

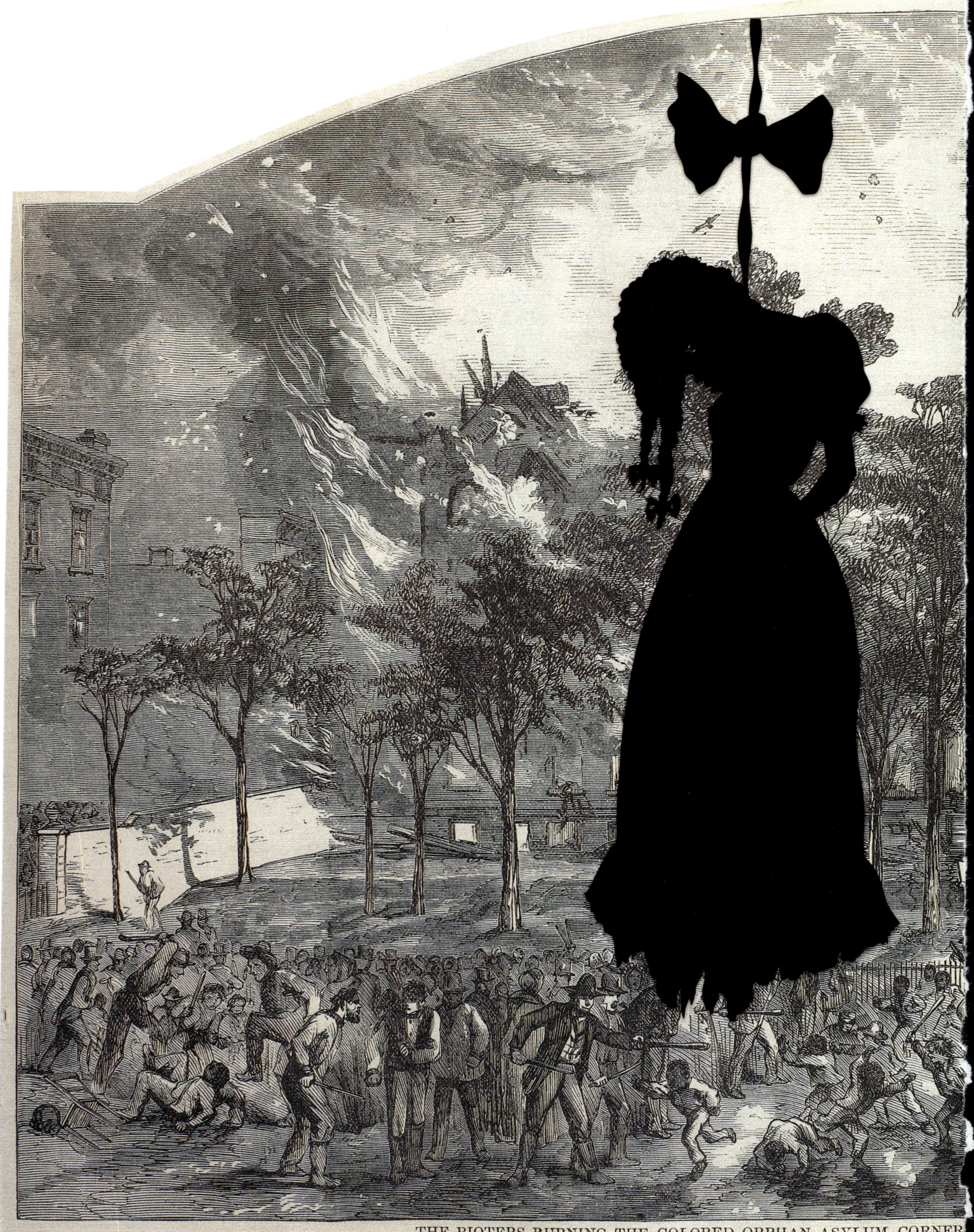

THE RIOTERS BURNING THE COLORED ORPHAN ASYLUM, CORNER

be appliquéd onto the tapestry', says Walker. 'I want it to be made from a different material, something black and lush – possibly velvet – but that hasn't been decided yet.'

Black humour makes the barbarities portrayed in her cut-outs easier to digest, but with nothing to ameliorate the horror of this scene, one tends to respond with numbed shock. 'There's nothing funny about it', says Walker, 'except that the level of cruelty it shows borders on the absurd. I couldn't find a way to embellish the print except to enlarge it. The incident happened in the civil war during the draft riots, which were provoked by poverty, racism and tensions over immigration. This was a revenge attack on the city's most vulnerable inhabitants.' Why did she choose this image for the tapestry? 'I didn't know about the event until a few years ago when I was thumbing through *Harper's Pictorial History*... and I wanted to bring it alive, to give it a domestic presence. It's how wars go, and are still going on. 9/11 is still a big deal here.'

Walker loves history paintings, because of the way they dramatise the past and portray each incident from the victor's point of view, as a moment of heroic achievement.[2] 'They're funny because they're so over the top', says Walker. 'They're an attempt to represent history, but it seems there's not much truth in them.' Made for a wealthy elite, tapestries have often served a similar function. 'Newspaper reports are very different, though', Walker points out. 'They are supposedly accurate. And the engraving, which is an early example of mass-media information, is very crude. It has a clunky humbleness and I liked the irony of transferring this lowly craft into a medium once used for kings and princes. There's also an unwitting humility about the cut-out silhouette. It's an undervalued craft form, considered second rate and second class; it isn't serious art.' Does her need to uncover the past work in a similar way to the truth and reconciliation hearings in South Africa, I wonder? Is it a matter of confronting American history, in order to allow the process of forgiveness to begin?

'It seems to go that way', says Walker, 'except that I have a trickster view. I get things out in the air and then I embellish them, because I'm a painter, for God sake! It's what I do. If I was writing history it would be a whole different thing.'

I imagine her work is very hands on. 'I have a few people who help out in the studio', she says. 'So sending things off is very disconcerting and I feel disconnected from the project. I ask myself "What have I done?" But I'm looking forward to the moment when I see the finished work. I like to be hands-on and know what I'm doing – to see how things function. How does a tapestry differ from a wall installation, a painting or a film? Is it a wall hanging or does it divide a room? Without that I feel a bit out of the loop.'[3]

[1] In an interview with *Art 21* 'The Melodrama of "Gone with the Wind"', 2003.
[2] In American art, events are usually shown from the white man's perspective.
[3] Unless otherwise stated, all comments by the artists in these texts were made in conversation with the author.

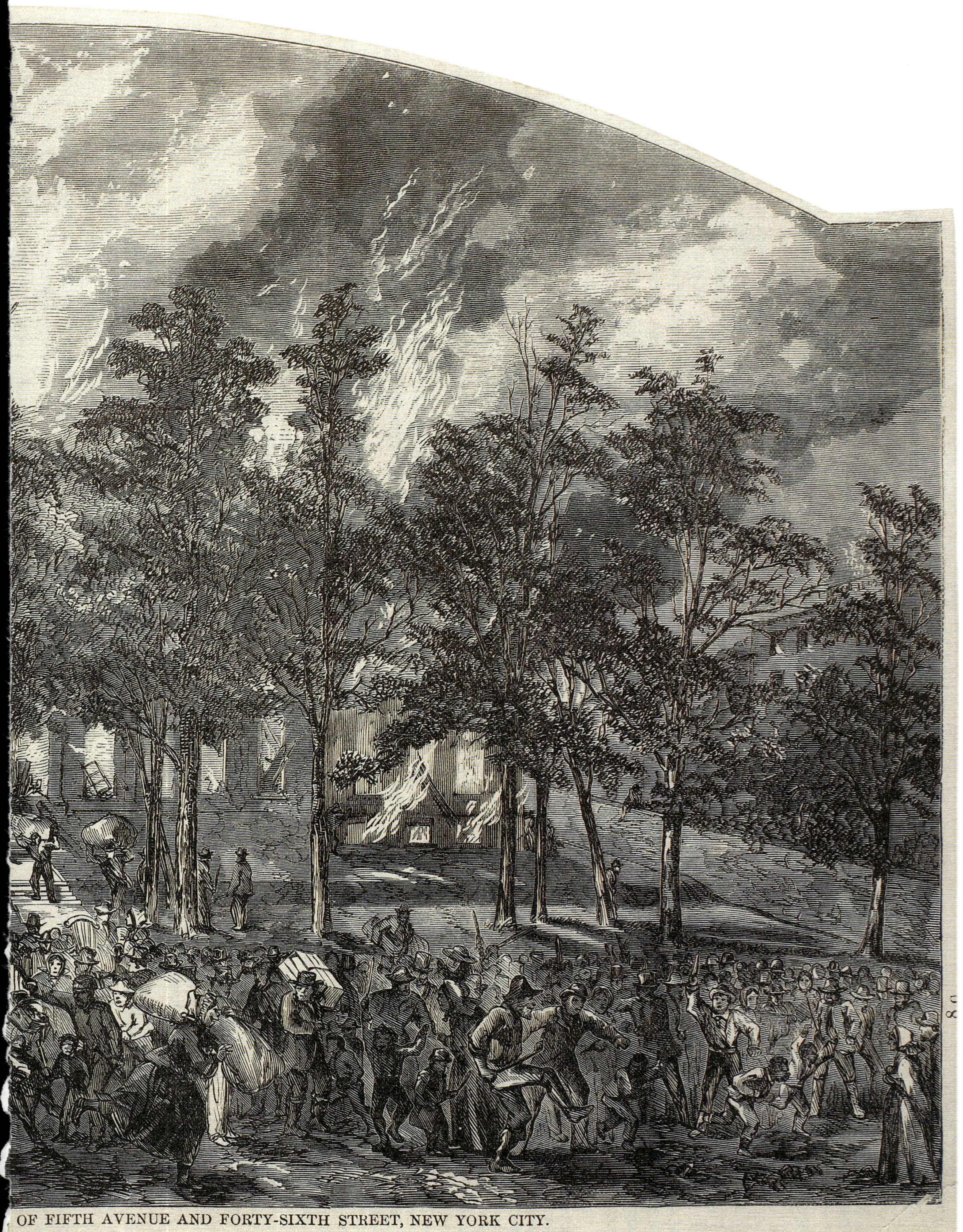

OF FIFTH AVENUE AND FORTY-SIXTH STREET, NEW YORK CITY.

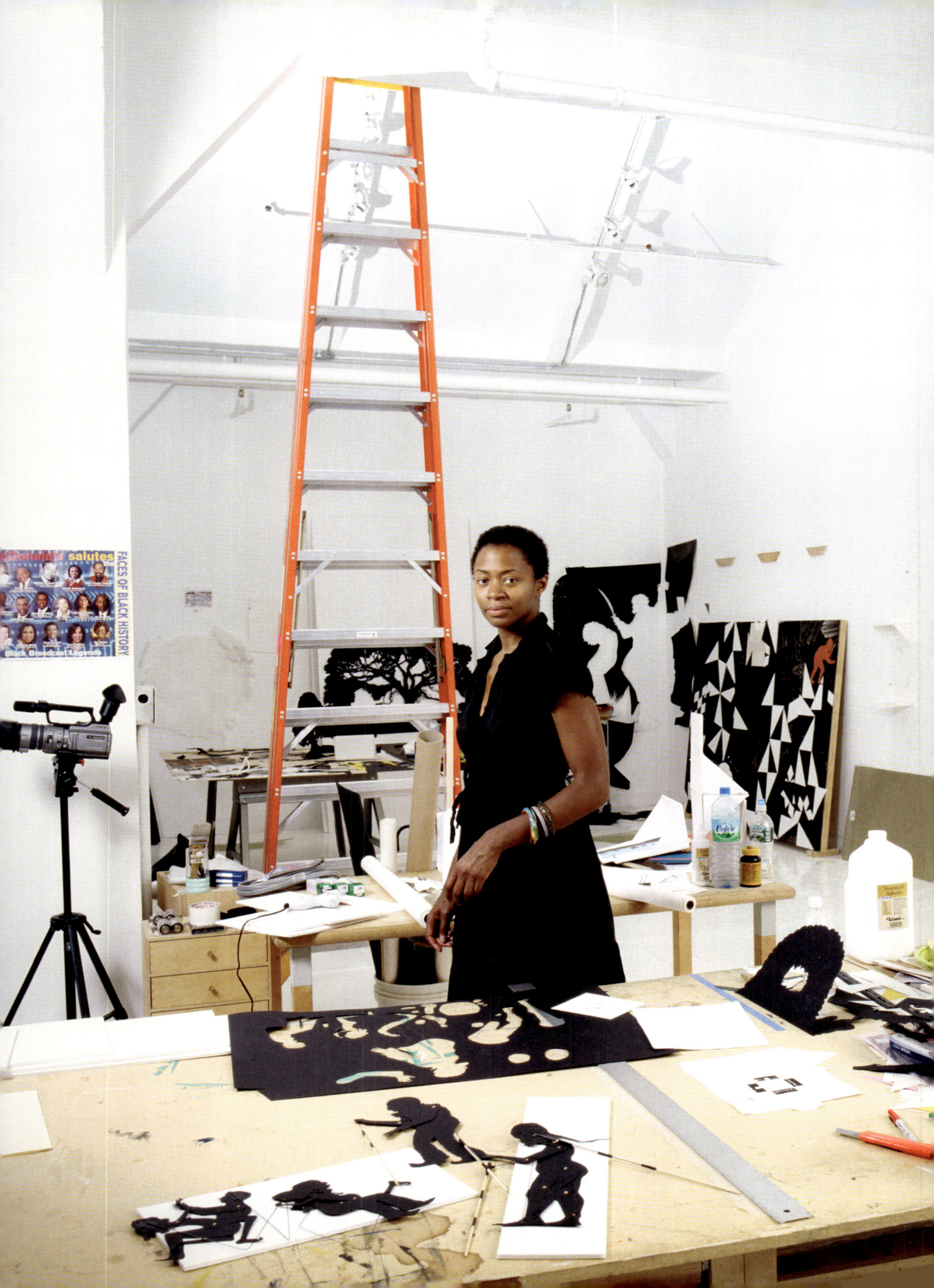
cDonald's salutes
FACES OF BLACK HISTORY
Black Broadcast Legends

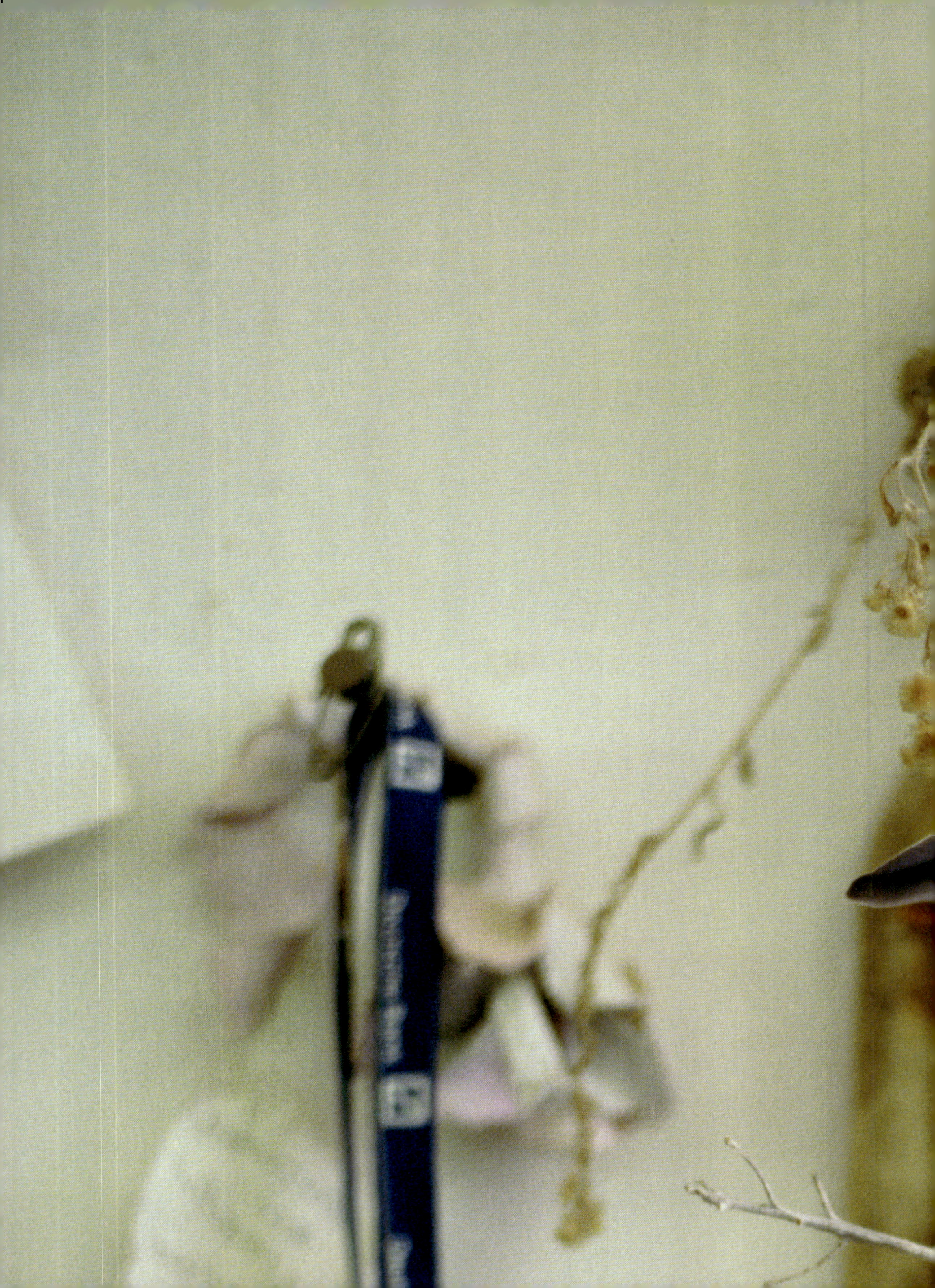

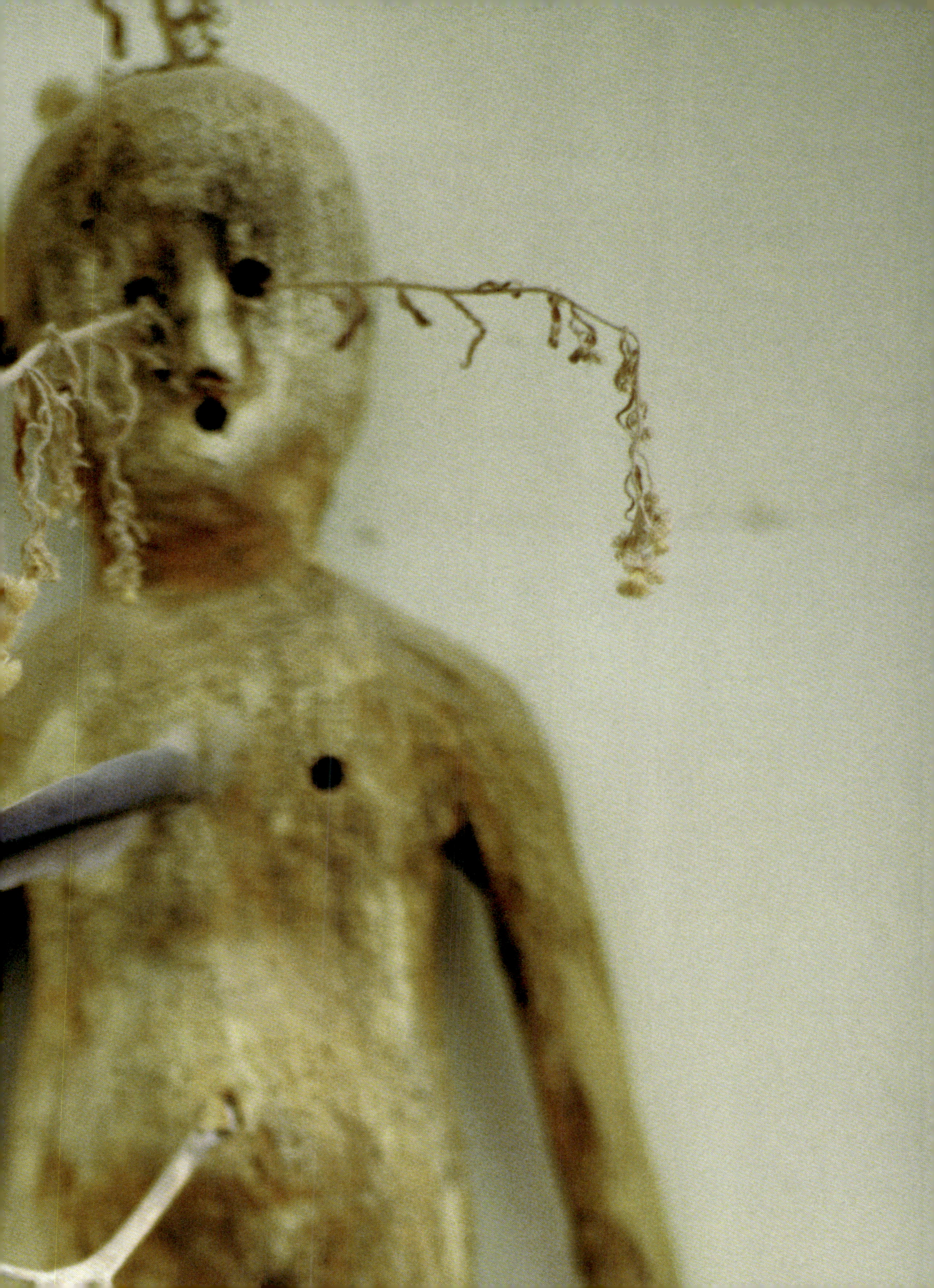

Vote Alan Measles For God
Grayson Perry

'Vote Alan Measles For God, He Will Save Us' reads the
message running along the top and bottom of Grayson
Perry's tapestry. The design is dominated by Alan
Measles, the teddy bear the artist has cherished since
childhood. Balancing precariously atop New York's Twin
Towers, the demented bear brandishes a kalashnikov and
strapped round his waist is a suicide belt. His teeth bared
in a murderous grimace, he urges us to join the fight, but
against whom? It's not clear whose side he is on.

Aircraft crash into both Twin Towers as the anonymous
falling man hurtles to the ground. At the foot of the
towers lies the Pentagon, and this American enclave
is separated from the rest of the mayhem by Israel's
security fence. From a television screen, Osama Bin
Laden gives his blessing to numerous acts of carnage.
A United Nations car explodes, a Molotov cocktail
burns, helicopters and fighter jets fill the air while, down
below, coffins, body bags and tombstones occupy every
available inch.

The rabble-rousing Alan Measles clearly owes his
allegiance to violence. It's in his blood, literally; his veins
sprout hand grenades and his blood-lust is causing an
erection. Peace is not even a glimmer on the horizon.
Perry's alter ego, Claire appears in a blue frock, wings
outstretched and pigtails flying; but she seems more like
a spirit of death than an angel of rebirth.

Alan Measles is blood red and the colours – maroon,
navy, dusty pink, grey, mauve and black against a
harvest yellow ground – remind one of those used in
Afghan rugs. The sides of the tapestry are decorated
with a fringe, as though this were indeed a carpet.
'I wanted a palette of natural dyes so I specified the
colours very closely', Perry explains. 'The design was
inspired by Afghan war rugs; I've got several of them
on my floor at home. They started making them in the
1980s in response to the Russian invasion; they look
very traditional but they feature helicopters, missile
launchers and kalashnikovs, and there's often a map

Vote Alan Measles For God
2.5 x 2m (8ft 2in x 6ft 7in)
Wool needlepoint, 2008

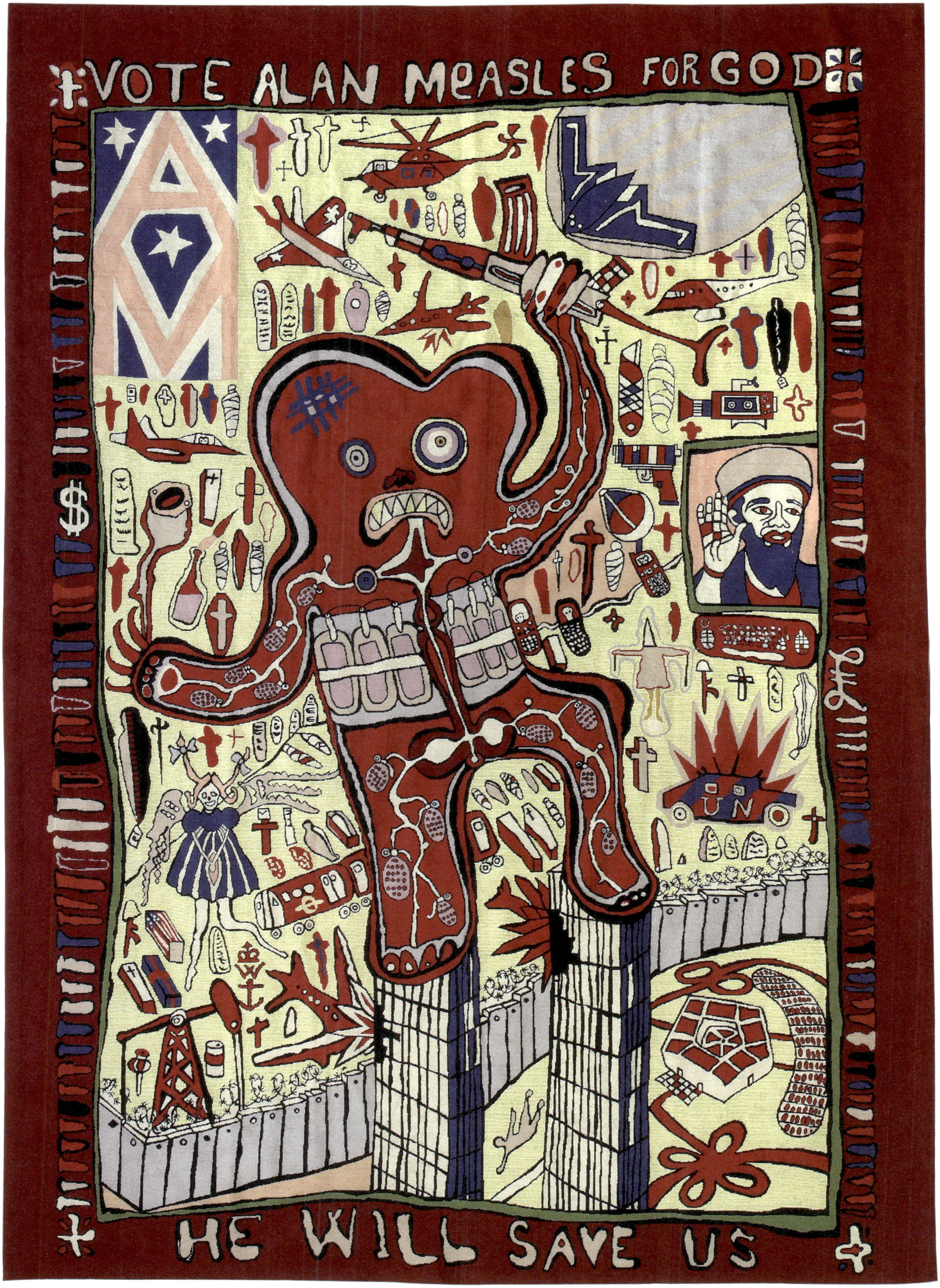

VOTE ALAN MeASLES FOR GOD
HE WILL SAVE US
AM
UN

of Afghanistan. The irony is that they sold them to the soldiers fighting the Mujahadin in order to raise funds for the Mujahadin. Now they've become tourist souvenirs.' Did he enjoy designing the tapestry? 'It was a great opportunity to work large', he says. 'I wanted a banner-like quality; I was thinking about political posters and trades union banners, of which we have a long tradition in Britain, and appliquéd quilts from the United States. I'm interested in folk artefacts, in general; it's the main starting point for all my work.'

Perry, who won the Turner Prize in 2003, is best known for his hand-coiled pots. From a distance they appear decorative; close to, though, one discovers that the images covering the surface are angry reflections on cruelty, inequality and injustice as well as recollections of an unhappy childhood, during which Alan Measles often seemed like his only ally.

'Alan Measles was my surrogate father', Perry explains, 'the coalescence of all maleness; I thought of him as a leader or guerilla fighter. He resisted the invasion of the Germans, for instance, when they arrived in the form of my step-father. If you look at people's biographies, you discover that dictators are often playing out their own childhood dramas on everyone else. Alan Measles is the acknowledgment of that; in the tapestry, I'm relating my imaginary, childhood world to the wider world. My creativity is rather mischievous; the black humour is always there, but it's a positive force. Humour is a good medium for kicking up issues without being too ernest or po-faced.'

Perry often appears in public as Claire, a young girl dressed in elaborate party frocks which he designs himself. 'One of the reasons I dress up as a woman', he has said, 'is my low self-esteem, to go with the image of women being seen as second class.... it is like pottery: that is seen as a second-class thing to do.'[1] The frocks provide an opportunity for him to explore his interest in fabrics, dress design and embroidery.

'I've often used embroidery and appliqué in my costumes and quilts', he says. 'I designed a sampler, for instance, which reads "You will die / You are alone / There is no God / Upon his throne". It's a kind of humanist prayer, an update of those Adam and Eve samplers from the nineteenth century. I've always used computerised embroidery, which has a slightly impersonal feel. I found a company in Holland that can do it digitally; you simply press a button and turn it out. But I really like the irregularities of the hand-made product.

'I drew the design half scale, then scanned it into a computer and used Photoshop to colour it in. In the process, some of the pixels came out the wrong colour; but when I blew the image up I left the mistakes in and the weavers have converted these digital errors into handmade ones, which I really like. The quality of the finished tapestry is amazing. I like the variety of the stitching; they've used cross-stitching which, in some sections, is very bold and in others really fine.'

[1] Quoted by Katharine Stout in the Turner Prize brochure, 2003.

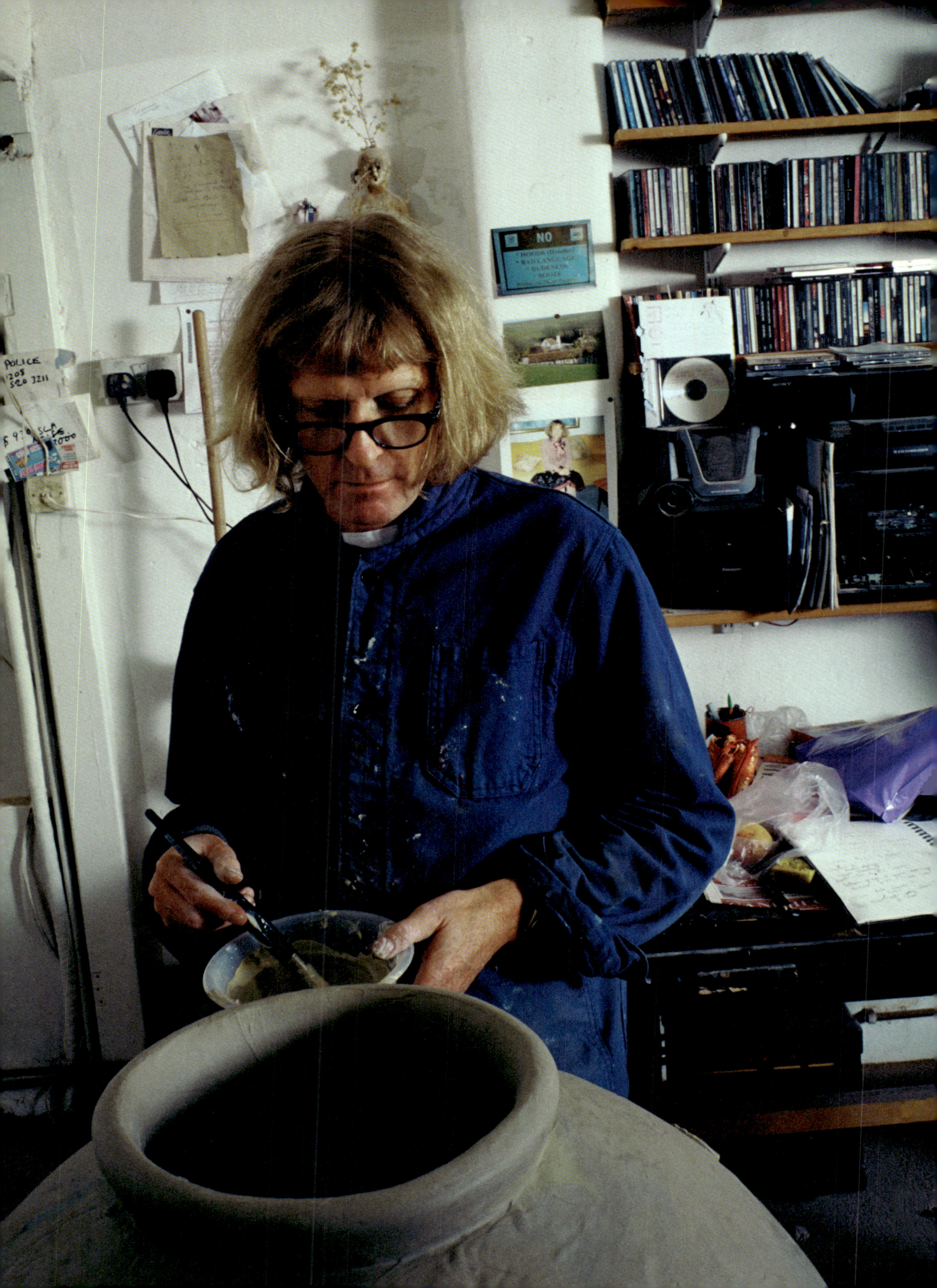

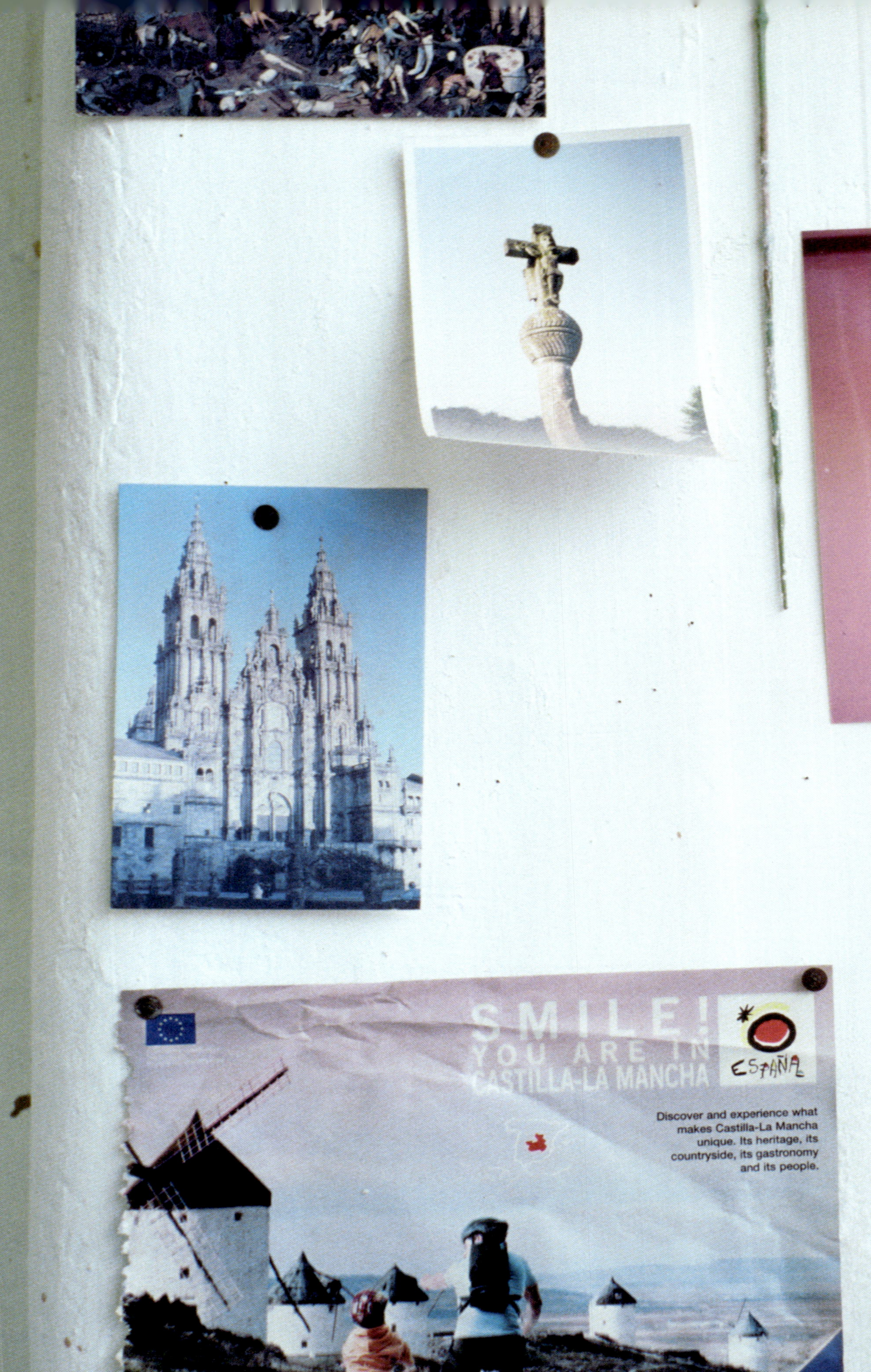
SMILE!
YOU ARE IN
CASTILLA-LA MANCHA
ESPAÑA
Discover and experience what
makes Castilla-La Mancha
unique. Its heritage, its
countryside, its gastronomy
and its people.

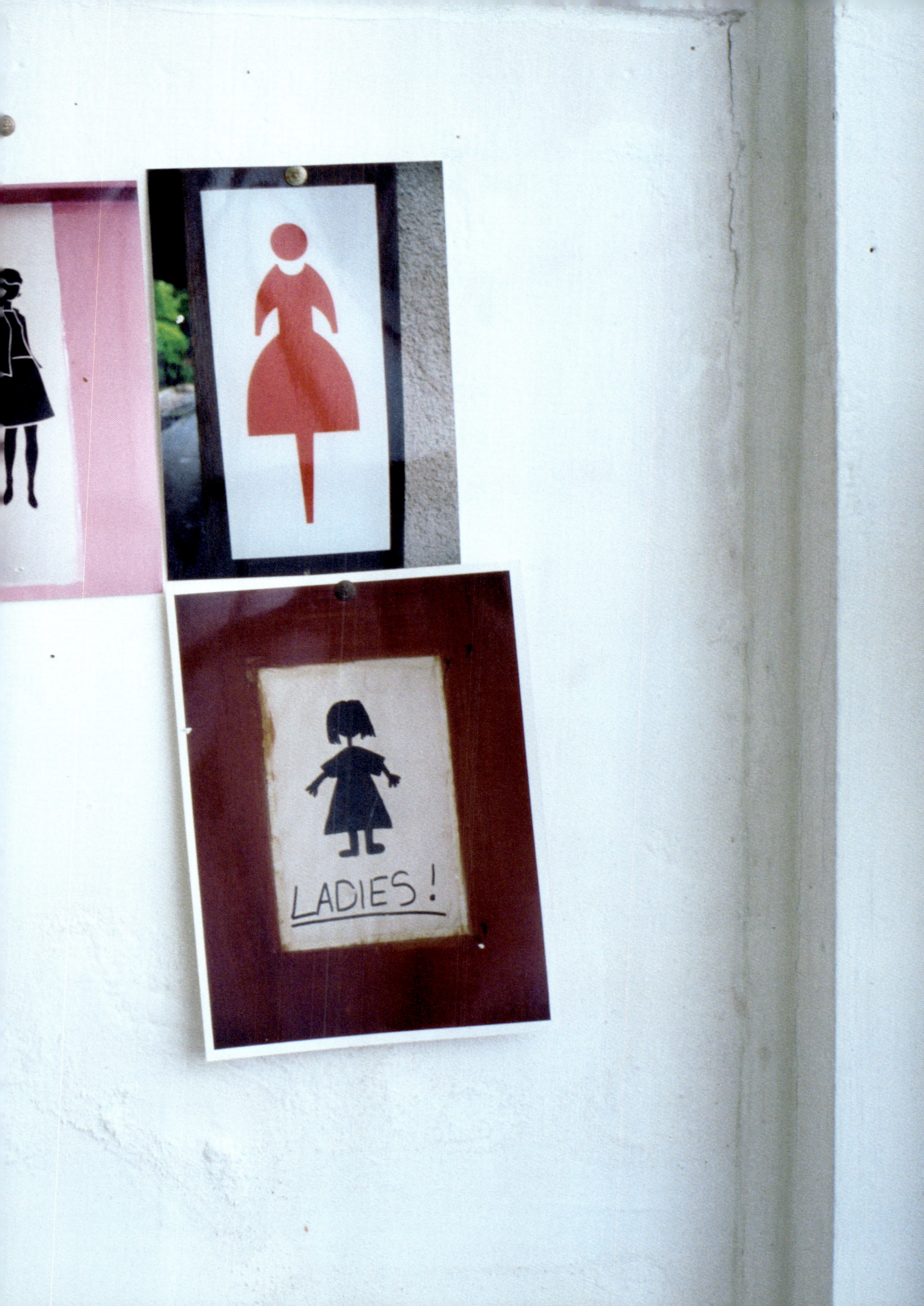
LADIES!

Carioca
Beatriz Milhazes

Beatriz Milhazes' paintings are exuberant celebrations of pattern and colour. 'Imagine a firework display frozen at a moment of explosive ecstasy and you get some idea of the orgiastic splendour of the work', I wrote in *Time Out* magazine.[1] 'Opaque colours contrast with translucent washes through which you can see layers of underpainting' I continued. 'Some areas look stencilled on, others have been transferred from sheets of plastic which, when peeled away, take some of the paint with them leaving surfaces that look cracked and peeling. The imperfections introduce a sense of time... an awareness of the making process: the accretion of countless decisions (false moves, corrections and flourishes) required to produce a painting.'

'My painting is a lot about process', confirms Milhazes. 'I don't make preparatory sketches or drawings. I may have images and colours in mind, but the way I work is very open – of the moment. I usually make work for a particular context or show, and I like to introduce new problems and questions each time. I'm interested in images that are optically disturbing and for a long time I've used circles to explore this, because they produce the sensation of movement. But I couldn't generate the same impression with straight lines so, in 2002/3, I began tackling the question of how to make paintings using squares and stripes. And I managed to open new doors and develop new compositions.'

Being used to working spontaneously and making constant adjustments and modifications, it must have been difficult for her to arrive at a design for the tapestry? 'Every medium has different requirements', she says, 'and rather than simply transferring the process I use in painting, I like to have a dialogue with each medium and take advantage of the possibilities it offers. I am often asked to design clothes, textiles and architectural ornament, but I don't normally accept because the offers are too limited in scope. Recently I've been working on projects for buildings, though. In 2004, I did a design for the facade of Selfridges in

Carioca
2 x 2m (6ft 7in x 6ft 7in)
Wool background, silk floral motif, tapestry, 2008

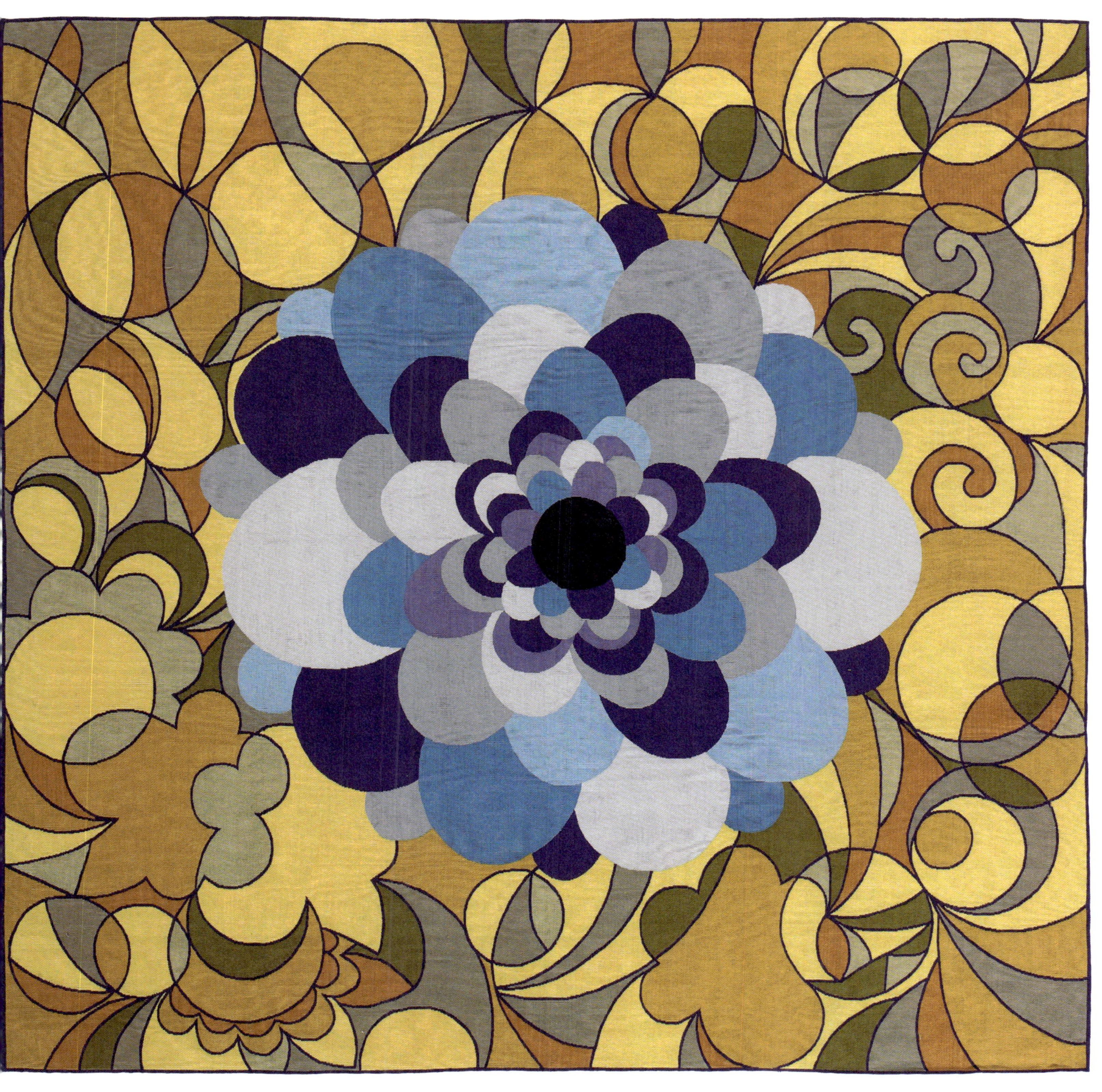

Manchester which was really a challenge, because it was so much bigger than the original drawings. It was seven stories high – like an infinite painting – and had to be really simple. The following year, I did the murals for Gloucester Road station and for the restaurant at Tate Modern and I've just finished a project with the architect Philippe Starck for Taschen's bookstore in New York. They all have some connection to tapestry.'

In the murals, saturated colours, overlapping circles and flower-like forms create a carnival mood that evokes the speed and energy of life in Rio de Janeiro where Milhazes lives. In her tapestry, the background consists of a similarly restless design of overlapping circles that implies constant flux and change while, paradoxically, appearing static and fixed. 'The structure of my work is very rational', she explains. 'It's based on geometry, but I was thinking about organic movement and circulation. I did the design by hand, on paper, and the circles were drawn with very freehand movements. The drawing is quite small, about 50 centimetres square (18 inches); my assistant scanned it into a computer and scaled it up. I couldn't change the image afterwards, so it had to work as a graphic response.'

Ranging from ochres to rust, olive and grey, the autumnal colours of the tapestry are more sober, more English, than the vibrant palette she normally uses. Separated by fine purple lines, the interlocking shapes look like pieces of variously coloured wood inlaid in a marquetry panel. The purple also establishes a visual link with the purple, blue and grey silk petals of the large, central flower. The colour and density of the design remind me of wallpapers and textiles produced by William Morris. Was it her intention to refer to English pattern-making? 'Not really', she says. 'What excited me about the tapestry was the opportunity to experience new possibilities, to draw a design for a completely different medium. I look at textile designs in general, though, and sometimes ideas emerge from them, and the colour combinations were consciously influenced by them.'

Is she happy with the way the colours have come out? 'Recently I was invited to design some upholstery fabric for a company in New York called Mahara. I was aware that one would have to compromise and I'm open to discussion, but the printed colours were so different from the originals! For the tapestry, though, they were able to dye the thread specially and reproduce all the colours I suggested; the range is almost the same. I only changed one small thing – and that was because I wanted to, rather than because they got it wrong!'

[1] *Time Out* issue 1842. 7.12.05.

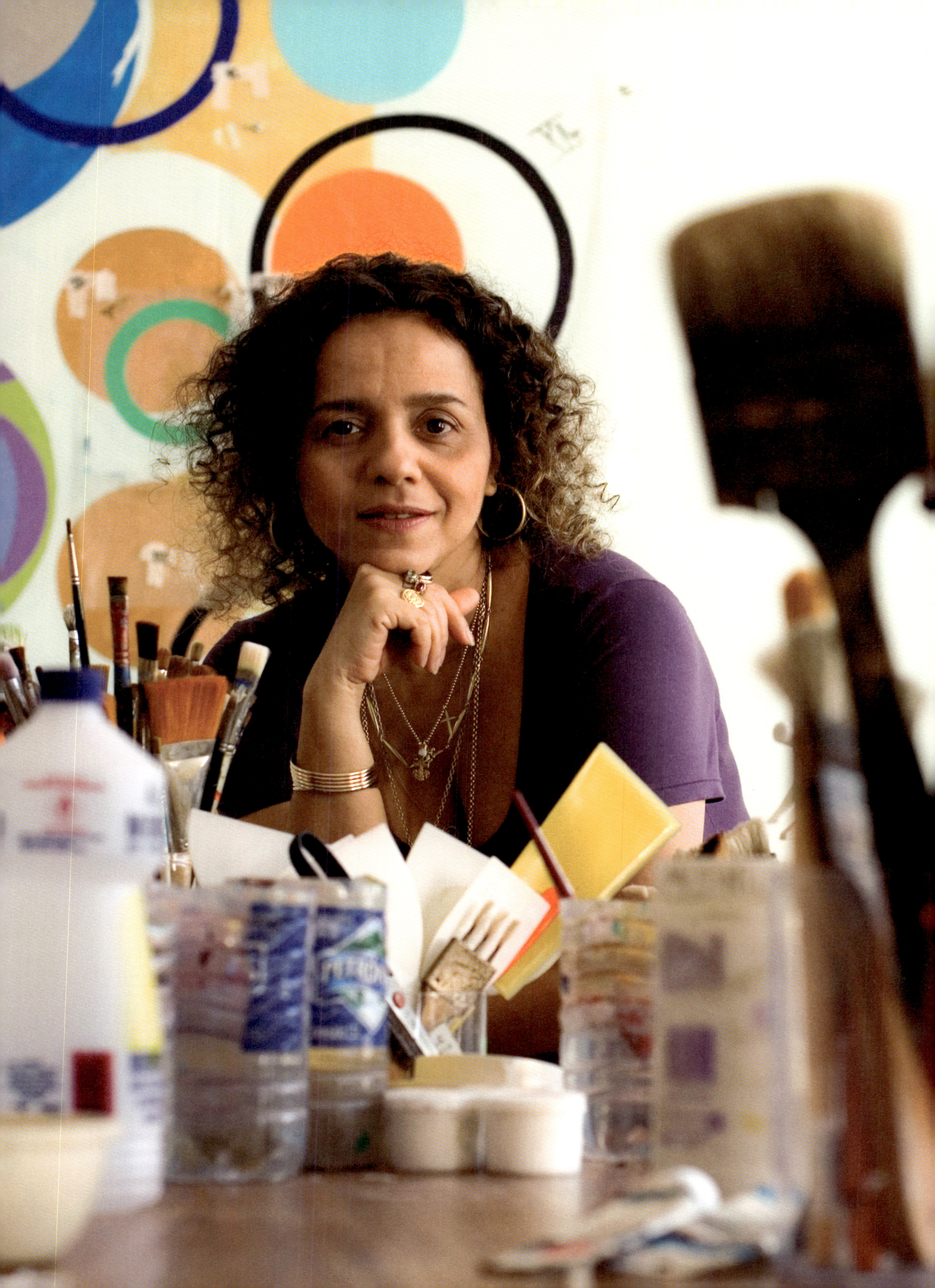

After Migrant Fruit Thugs
Fred Tomaselli

Fred Tomaselli's tapestry is based on an existing work
that features two large birds perched on the branches
of a fig tree. Their plumage has been replaced by a
myriad of eyes and flowers in subtle shades of rose,
magenta, mauve, blue and gold. Surrounding these
exotic thieves are actual fig leaves and jewel-like fruits
that dangle invitingly from the branches like purple
tear drops. It is night and the blue-black sky twinkles
with heavenly bodies shaped like snow flake crystals,
starburst brooches and Christmas tree decorations. The
various elements are suspended in resin, which gives the
work an extraordinary depth and richness of colour. 'My
resin-paint-collages read as pure painting from across
the room', Tomaselli has said, 'but when you get right
up close to them, you find that they're composed of a
multitude of bits that combine the real, the photographic
and the painterly.'[1]

An avid collector, Tomaselli has amassed a vast archive
of images cut from books and magazines – noses, eyes,
mouths, ears and other body parts as well as birds,
butterflies, moths and reptiles, which provide the raw
material for his exquisite assemblages. 'I consider myself
a maximalist artist', he has said, 'in that I try to throw
as much information into an object as it can physically
handle.'[2]

As a child he had a 'low-rent garage zoo that housed
various creepy animals including scorpions, tarantulas,
lizards, frogs and snakes all of which I would catch
around my neighbourhood. Now that I'm a middle-aged
family man... my studio is a continuation of my garage
and my garden provides me with the collection of plants
that find their way into my work.'[1]

When I talk to him on the phone, Tomaselli is bird
watching in the Placerita Canyon, a nature reserve just
outside Los Angeles; the conversation is punctuated by
whoops of delight: 'Oh my God, I've just seen a red-
shouldered hawk! There's a white-breasted nuthatch!
That's a lazuli bunting!' When it comes to bird watching,

After Migrant Fruit Thugs
2.5 x 1.6m (8ft 2in x 5ft 4in)
Wool background, silk birds
with metallic thread detail, 2008

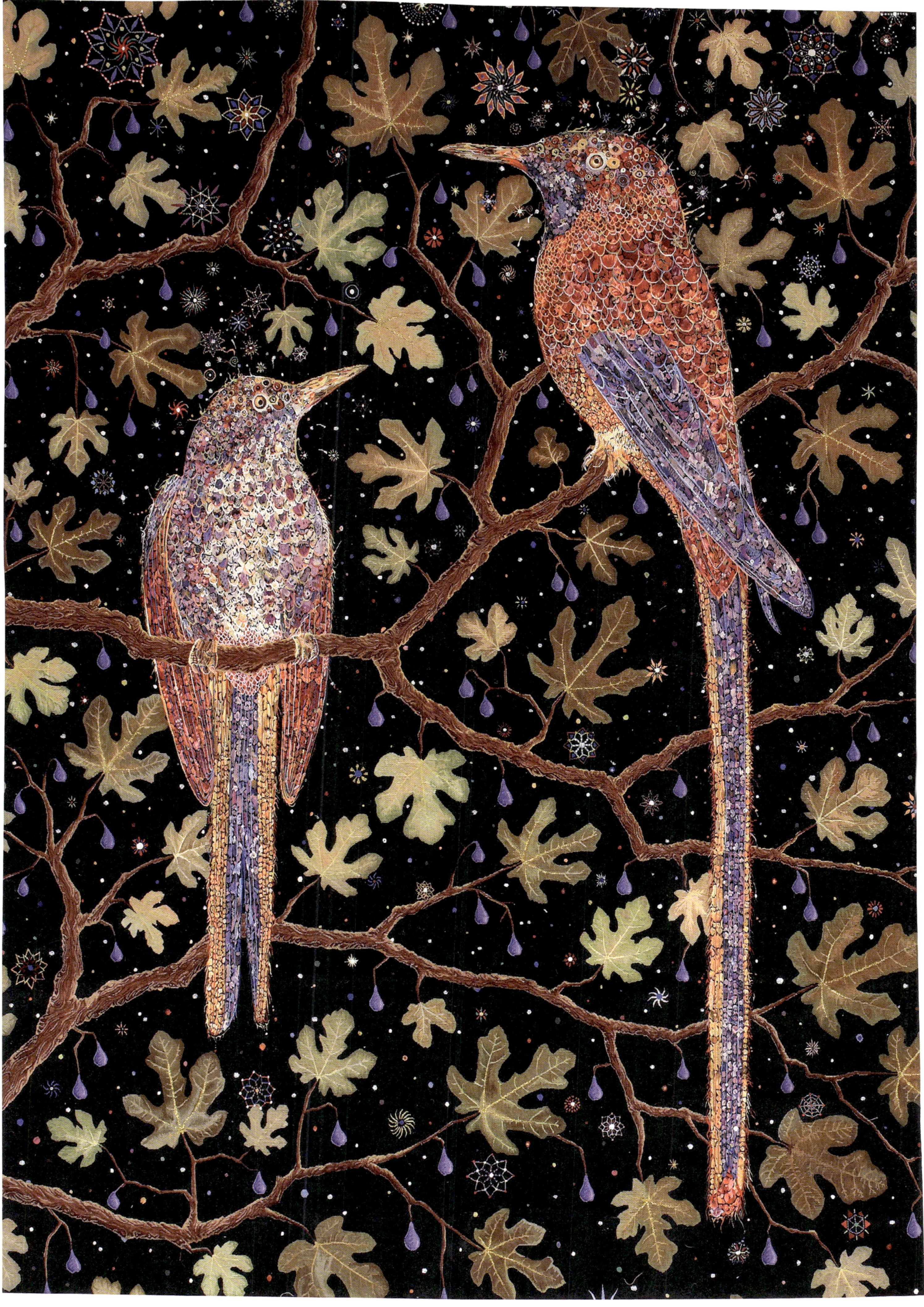

though, he claims to be 'a bad amateur... I do it on
my own because I find bird watchers boring – they're
obsessive, compulsive.'

Nor does he draw or photograph birds. The exotic pair in
the tapestry are honey-creepers from New Guinea, which
he has never seen. 'I just use pictures from books', he
explains. 'I liked the long tails and scalloping feathers and
I borrowed the anatomical structure as a shape within
which to hang some ornament; I was playing around and
free-associating – having fun. Birds can seem fantastical
and hallucinatory. When I saw a hooded oriole for the
first time, it seemed other-worldly; I was transported
into another place. But real birds are not made of flowers
and don't have a million eyes! I think it was Baudelaire
who said that the beautiful is always strange, and this
strangeness differentiates it from prettiness, which is an
ordinary thing.'

Growing up in Southern California, Tomaselli used to
make surfboards and their sleek, resin coated surfaces
gave him the idea of using the medium to stabilise the
ingredients in his assemblages. 'I love the seductive
finish of the resin', he says. 'These are like vehicles to
transport you to other places.'[2]

The tapestry weavers were unable to imitate the
transparent sheen of the resin, but the birds are woven
in silk thread which glistens against the wool of the richly
dark ground; gold thread infiltrates the veins of the fig
leaves and illuminates the stars and festive decorations.
These remind me of bead and crochet work, especially
the intricate decorations made in Czechoslovakia to
celebrate Christmas. 'My interest in ornament extends
to all cultures', says Tomaselli, 'Indian, Tibetan, Persian,
American Indian – all the archaic symbols and folk art
traditions of mankind – and also to psychedelic kitsch and
outsider art.

'My work has always had a relationship to crafts, such as
marquetry or tapestry; I've never differentiated between
the realms of art and craft, whether it be customising
cars or doing macramé. And I have always loved
tapestries – they're an ancient form of pixelation and
they've often been places from which I get inspiration
– but there's a huge difference between being inspired
by them and making one. As an artist I'm very hands
on; everything is done by me, by hand, with only one
assistant. All decisions are taken by me, so jobbing out
to a person whom I've never met and working in another
country gave me some pause.

'But it's interesting to have the forms articulated by such
great craftsmen. I can't imagine anyone in this country
who could do such a great job – it's really amazing! It's
an aspect of global culture – working with a company in
London that uses craftsmen in Asia; and now you are
talking to someone in Los Angeles who lives in New
York. It's one of the better aspects of globalisation!'

[1] In conversation with Siri Hustvedt, *Another Magazine* Autumn/Winter 2007.
[2] Art in Progress: Fred Tomaselli 2005, a video produced by the James Cohan Gallery.

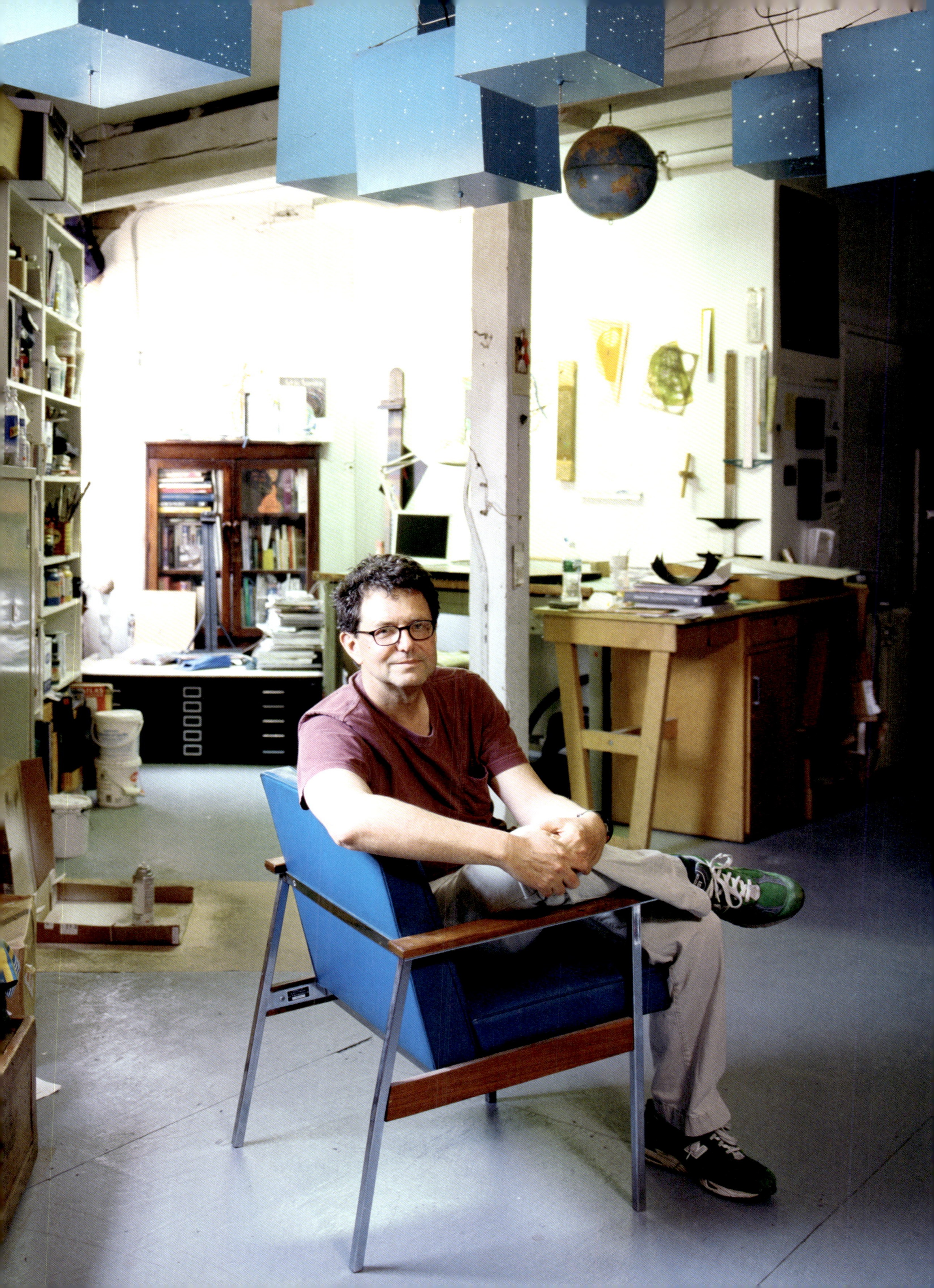

Ghada Amer & Reza Farkhondeh

Ghada Amer and Reza Farkhondeh have been working in the same studio for nearly twenty years and have recently embarked on a full-blown collaboration, in which their contributions remain quite distinct. 'He sees things in shapes and I see things in lines', Amer has said. 'My work tends to be quite systematic, but working with someone else gives me the possibility of breaking the system and going further.'[1] 'The Bugs and the Lovers' is from a series of drawings they made together in 2005. Stickers of a moth and various creepy crawlies including a ladybird, earwig, beetle, grass hopper and stick insect, are dotted around two pink roses painted in watercolour by Farkhondeh in such a way that the romantic associations of the flowers are compromised by their presence.

Areas of bare warp and weft create an outline of a couple having sex. Emphasis is on the woman's face and body; she appears to swoon in a transport of delight as she guides in her lover's penis and pleasures herself at the same time. The explicit nature of the image indicates that its source is a porn magazine. There's evident irony in Amer's choice of subject matter. 'It is an aberration to spend days sewing images of women taken from pornographic magazines for men', she says. 'I am participating in the double submission of the woman – the woman sewing and the woman sewing her own distorted image!... (but) I have no message to transmit, nothing to criticise or to denounce. This is maybe why I seem to have an ambiguous position, and I like to keep that impression.'[2]

Amer is best known for stitching similarly hard-core images onto canvas, where she allows the embroidery threads to trail down the surface like uncontrolled drips of paint, so hiding the erotic content behind a veil of silken tangles, while also disguising the embroidery as a painting. 'I liked the idea of representing women through the medium of thread because it is so identified with femininity', she says. 'I wanted to 'paint' a woman with embroidery too.' [1] Her desire to mimic painting with a

The Bugs and the Lovers
1.53 x 2.31m (5ft x 7ft 7in)
Wool tapestry with silk bugs, 2008

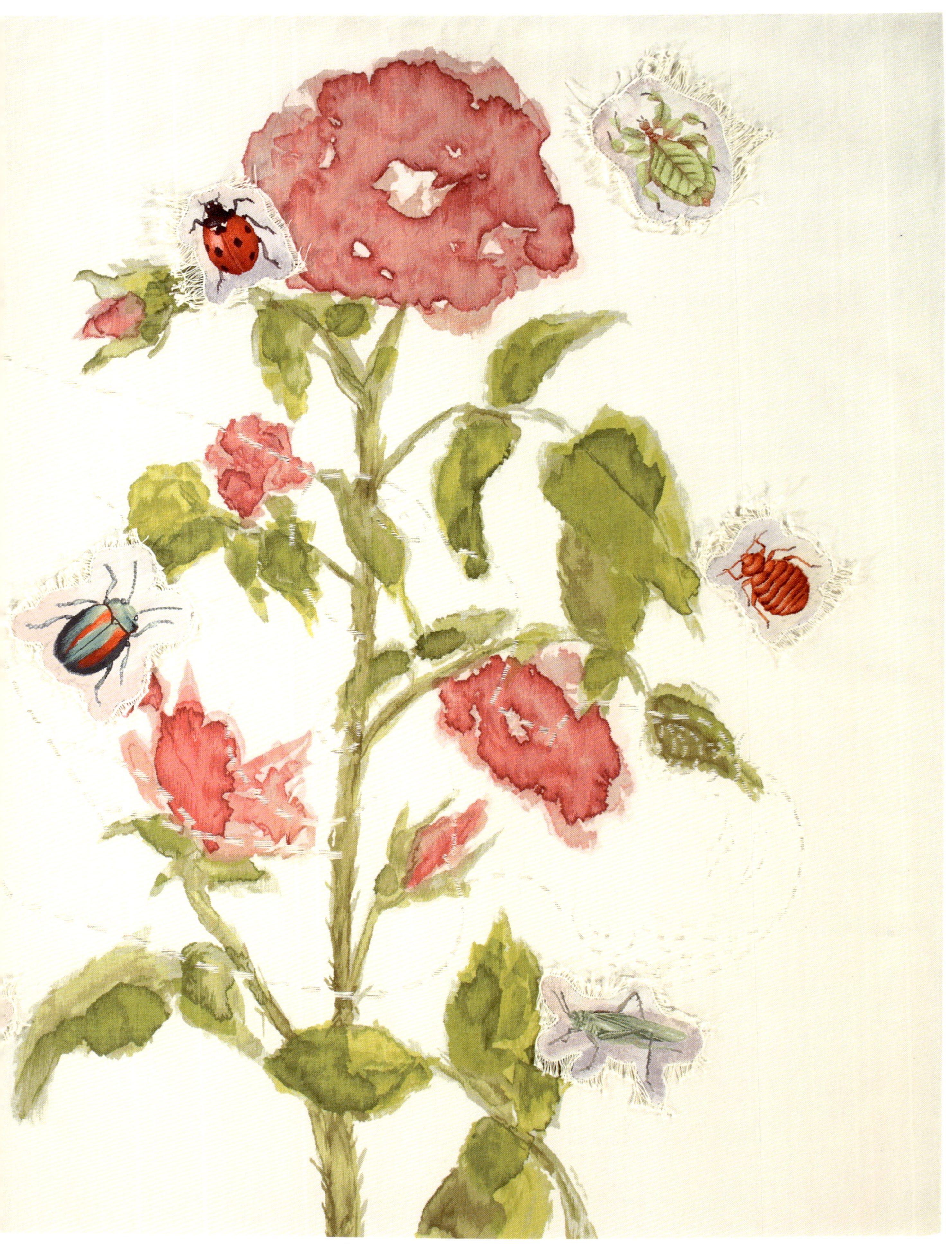

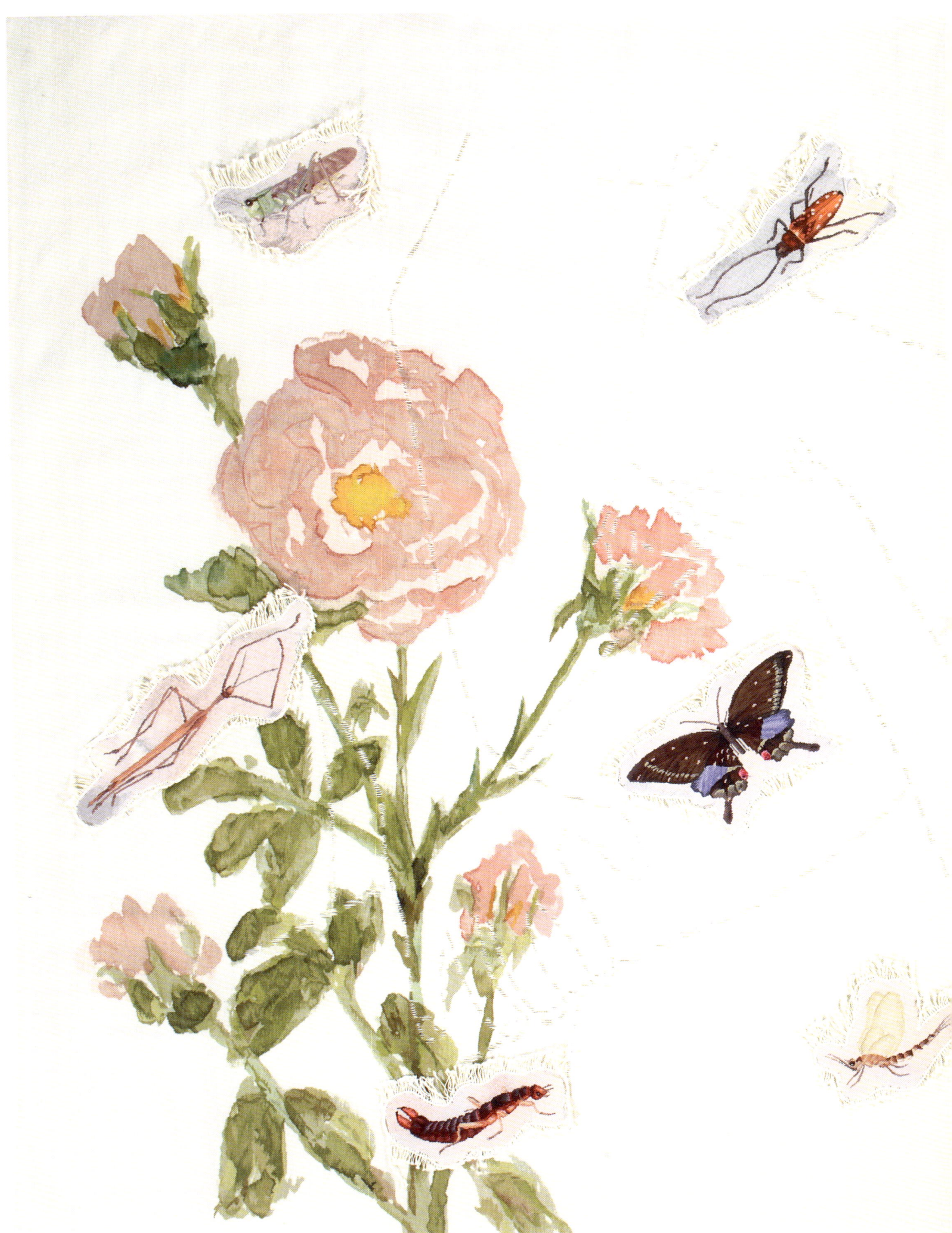

medium associated with women and also considered
a craft is an act of defiance that stems from her
experiences at the École des Beaux Arts in Nice, where
a male professor refused to teach female students the
'masculine' art of painting!

Because of its tendency to tear, she had difficulty
stitching through the paper and had to prick all the
holes with a needle before sewing the outline. This
machine-like way of working has produced a regular,
non-expressive outline that resembles one of those
dotted lines instructing one to 'cut-here' and makes the
figures appear even more generic and stereotypical. In
the drawing and the tapestry, two versions of sex – the
romantic and the literal – are juxtaposed as though to
contradict one another. 'Maybe it's not such a contrast',
says Amer. 'When you think about love as pure and
romantic, you forget about the love that is wild, difficult
and real. And as artists, we are asking questions rather
than giving answers.'

Is her way of working very hands-on? 'I get involved
in the craft aspect of the work but, rather than getting
bogged down in making things, I prefer to look for new
ideas and resolve new problems. So although I'm not a
conceptualist, I like to teach other people to do the work
for me; even my paintings are done with assistants.'

How does she feel about working in tapestry? 'I'm
not interested simply in transferring something to a
different medium', she says. 'What's the point? I think
differently with each change of medium. You can't
compare drawings and paintings, for instance; it's like
comparing apples and cucumbers, and both are different
from tapestry. We didn't want the weavers just to copy
the drawing, but to effect a transfer, to make a collage
of the different parts and put them together. The bugs,
for instance, will be woven separately in silk and then
attached to the tapestry around the flowers. We're
hoping the holes can be made on the loom by removing
some threads, but we don't know yet if it will work.'

[1] Quoted by Sonia Kolesnikov-Jessop, *International Herald Tribune* 3.12.2007.
[2] Interviewed by Xavier Franceschi, Francophone Art 2008.

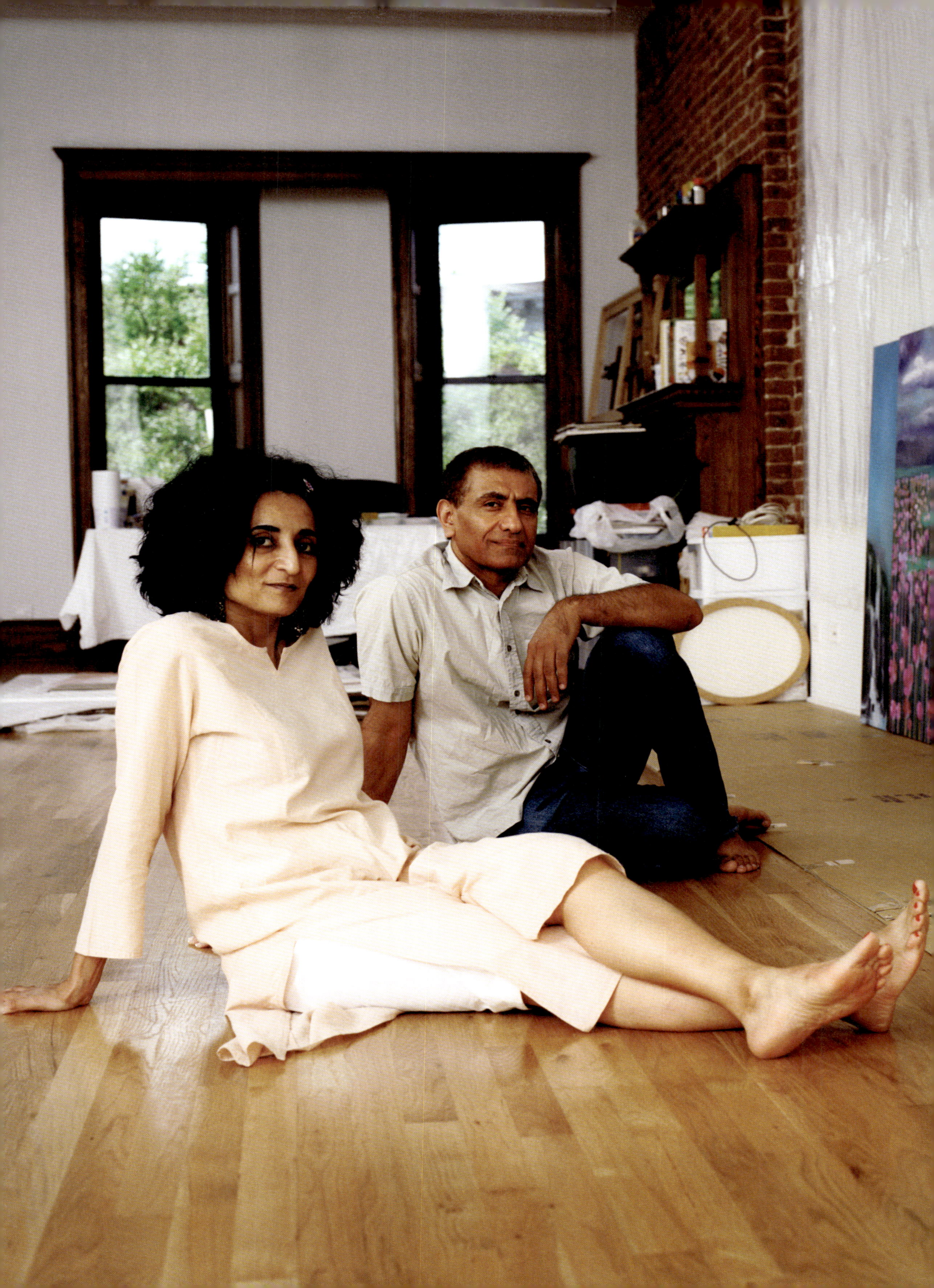

aaxé vatapá alegria feijão
avaf

avaf is a pseudonym for an artists' collective whose
core members are Eli Sudbrack, a Brazilian living in New
York, and French multimedia artist Christophe Hamaide-
Pierson. avaf stands for 'assume vivid astro focus', an
amalgam of Throbbing Gristle's album title 'Assume
Power Focus' and 80's rock band Ultra Vivid Scene. The
music and club scenes have been an inspiration to avaf
ever since its formation in 2001, and play an important
role in the group's installations. In Tate Liverpool in 2005,
for example, they showed the 'Butch Queen Realness
with a Twist in Pastel Colours Video Show', a compilation
of material pirated from the net or found on eBay,
which includes bootlegged copies of music videos and
television shows, artists' videos and performances, and
footage of club nights and vogue balls interspersed with
abstract designs and animations. A lot of research goes
into sourcing this material and avaf used to issue 'To Do'
lists detailing their quests. One list, for instance, includes
references to Jefferson Airplane, American architecture,
Tibetan Thangka paintings and 'The Doors of Perception'
by Aldous Huxley.

Installations are their favoured artform because they
provide an all-encompassing experience that lends itself
to collective authorship and audience participation. 'We
want to be contaminated by other people', avaf have
said. 'We believe in generosity and equality, in sharing
and inclusiveness. How many people are in the collective
varies according to the projects we are involved with.[1] If
you imagine 1960's psychedelia intensified to the power
of ten, it gives you some idea of the colour-drenched,
hippy-trippy visuals that avaf refer to as wallpaper and
with which they line the walls of their installations.

Given that light, sound and movement are such crucial
ingredients in their work, it seems strange that they
should agree to make a design for the archaic medium
of tapestry. 'Our big installations are made of a lot of
different elements including sculptures, wallpaper,
placards, videos, drawings, sound pieces and chain
curtains', avaf explain.[2] 'And tapestry could actually

aaxé vatapá alegria feijão
3.50 x 2.05m (11ft 6in x 6ft 8in)
Wool, silk and artificial silk tapestry,
with metallic thread detail, 2008

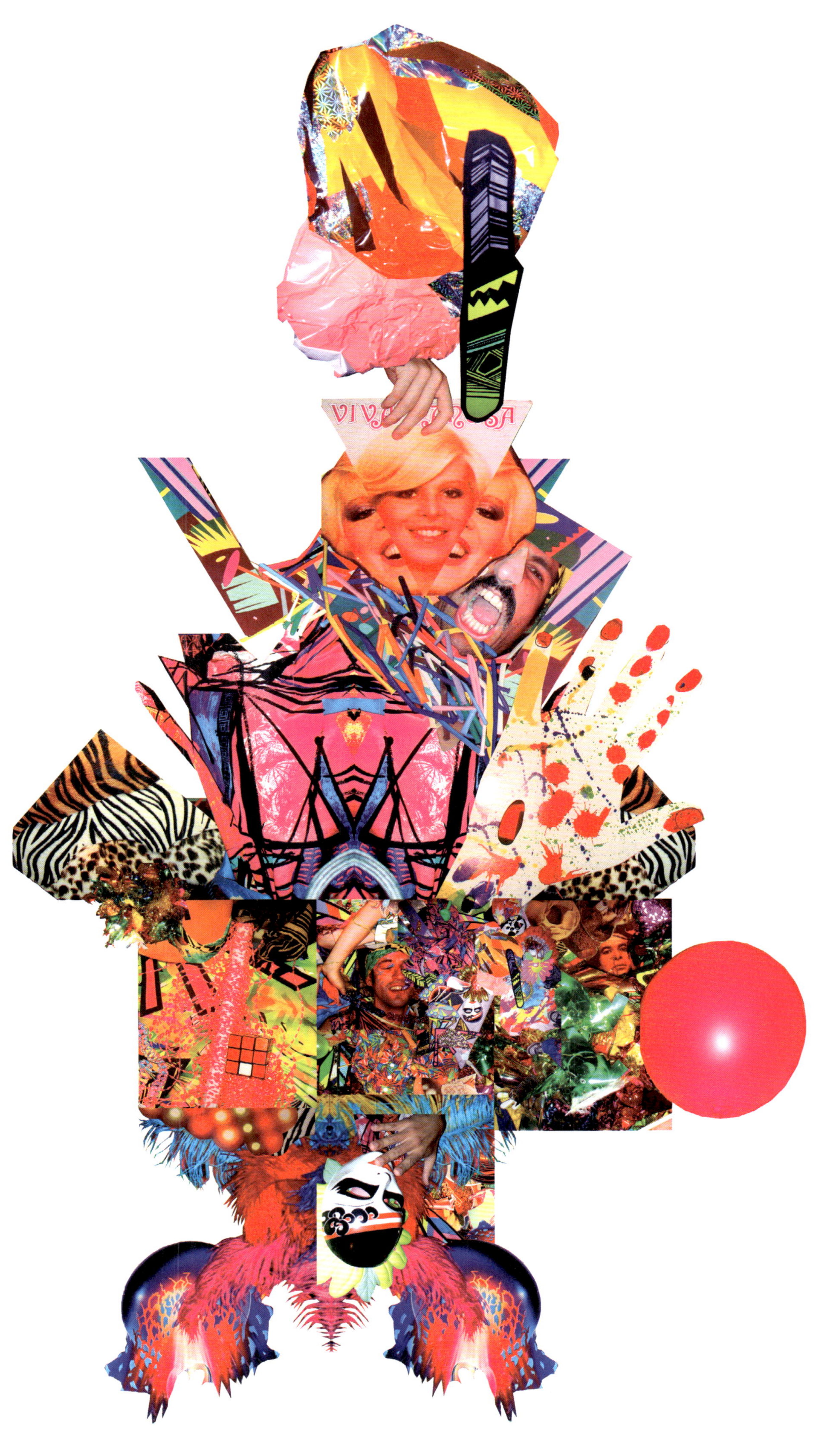

be one of the elements, because one of our earliest wallpaper pieces, 'GARDEN 1', was inspired by the famous tapestry 'The Lady and the Unicorn' in the Museum of the Middle Ages in Paris.[3] So being invited to create our own tapestry was quite special for us, because it was like going back to where it all started.

'The tapestry is called "aaxé vatapá alegria feijão",' they continue, 'which, as you've probably noticed, uses each initial of a.v.a.f. Coming up with new avaf meanings for each project is part of our new practice. It is an absurd sentence which is difficult to translate into English, but that suits this over-loaded, multi-layered tapestry project. Vatapà is a traditional Brazilian dish and feijão means 'bean' in Portuguese, so the title refers, in a metaphorical way, to our appetite for climactic collective happiness.'

Why is the tapestry shaped like a rocket? 'It was very important for us not to produce a tapestry in the usual rectangular shape', avaf explain. 'It was more challenging both for us and Banners of Persuasion to develop a shape that is more organic and more in sync with our art practice and, because there is a dynamic to it, this allows more ways to read the piece.'

The design is a collage of images that captures the hedonistic ethos both of carnival and of clubbing; they evoke the glory days of disco and gay activism. 'One of our concerns was to bring gay politics into the work', avaf have said, and previous installations have paid 'homage to the history of clubs and dance music and their close relationship to the birth of gay rights, at least in America. Clubs were not just simply hedonistic heavens, but spaces for unity within that community.'[1]

Members of avaf often wear masks to hide their identity and, in the tapestry, a masked figure trailing brightly coloured feather boas hitches a ride with the throng of revellers dancing their hearts out nearby. Are these images a record of previous avaf happenings? 'Most of the elements depicted in the tapestry', say avaf, 'were used or developed while we were in Brazil, especially during a private ceremony – an Abravanation-batucada. We and our collaborators – Neon, abravanation and 2 fanzine – gathered together and collected different material in order to create symbolic images. 2 fanzine, for instance, made the decorated hand, which is also a mask. So the tapestry is unique in that it represents the colourful burst of our collective Brazilian symbiosis experience.'

Does the work contain a political message of any kind? 'The political message', says avaf, 'lies in the fact that some of the images in the tapestry were created collectively, and we believe that being a collective force is a political act per se.'

[1] In an interview by Gerald Matt for avaf's *cheapcream* website 2006.
[2] My contact with avaf was by email.
[3] The mediaeval cycle known as 'The Lady and The Unicorn' consists of six tapestries respectively titled 'Love', 'Hearing', 'Sight', 'Touch', 'Smell' and 'Taste'. Featuring a lady, lion and unicorn in an exquisite formal garden, they are in the collection of the National Museum of the Middle Ages, Paris.

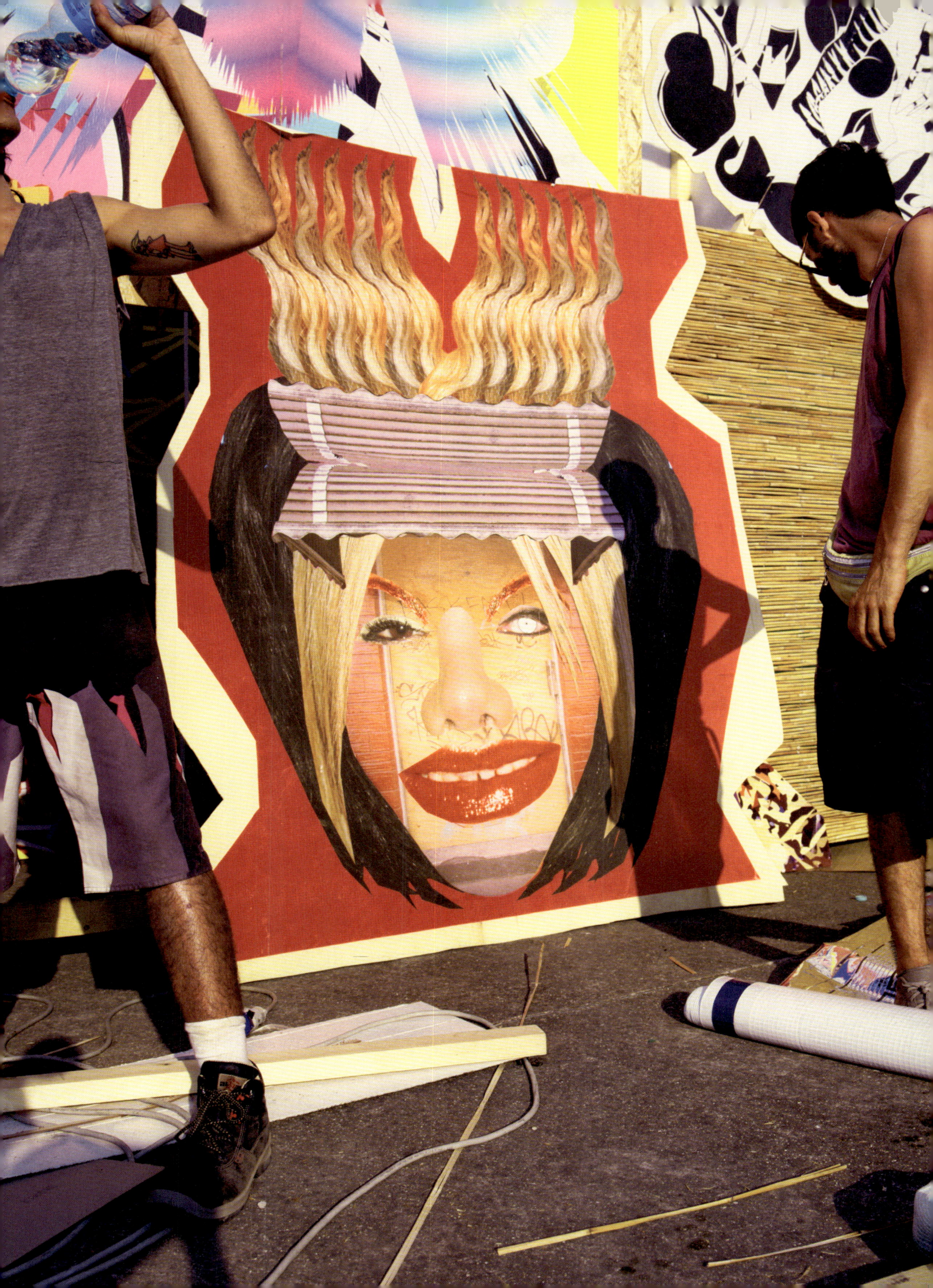

Mappa del Mundo
Gavin Turk

Gavin Turk's map of the world has been created from
discarded packaging and drink cans that have been run
over and squashed flat. 'I found them on the street near
a filling station', he tells me. 'I chose main brand sweets,
cigarettes and drinks rather than supermarket brands
– Ribena rather than Tesco's blackcurrant drink – so that
they are more generic and more global.

'When I was asked to design a tapestry all I could think
of was Alighiero Boetti's embroidered map of the world.[1]
I'd already made a world map out of crushed rubbish for
a project connected to Christian Aid. I photographed the
items, collaged them into a map of the world and then
sent a digital file of the image to a company that makes
globes. They divided the map into twelve segments and
wrapped it round a globe.

'I decided to use the same idea for the tapestry; I made
a full-size digital print of the collage, which is easy for the
weavers to work from because they can give a colour
value to each square. I haven't seen the finished tapestry
yet, but the rubbish should appear life size so that
everything will be recognisable, though the small text
will become more abstract. I want them to sew in some
shiny bits to create a sheen.'

In his map, the same brand names appear on every
continent and in every country – from Australia to
Greenland and Bosnia to Brazil. Is he making a point
about globalisation? 'I was thinking of the petrol station
as a source of travel from place to place, a means of
communication', he explains. 'Coca-Cola features quite a
bit because it is the best known coupling of words in the
world; it's the phrase most spoken abroad. There's no
correlation between the materials and the land masses,
though. The packaging looks a bit like rivers and valleys,
but only in a fanciful way. Which projection you decide to
use and how you prioritise certain countries is a political
battleground, though. I've lost the North Pole somehow
and cheated at the bottom. I've flattened out Antarctica
and made it huge, because I wanted a ragged edge.'

Mappa del Mundo
3.13 x 2m (10ft 3in x 6ft 7in)
Wool, silk and metallic thread tapestry, 2008

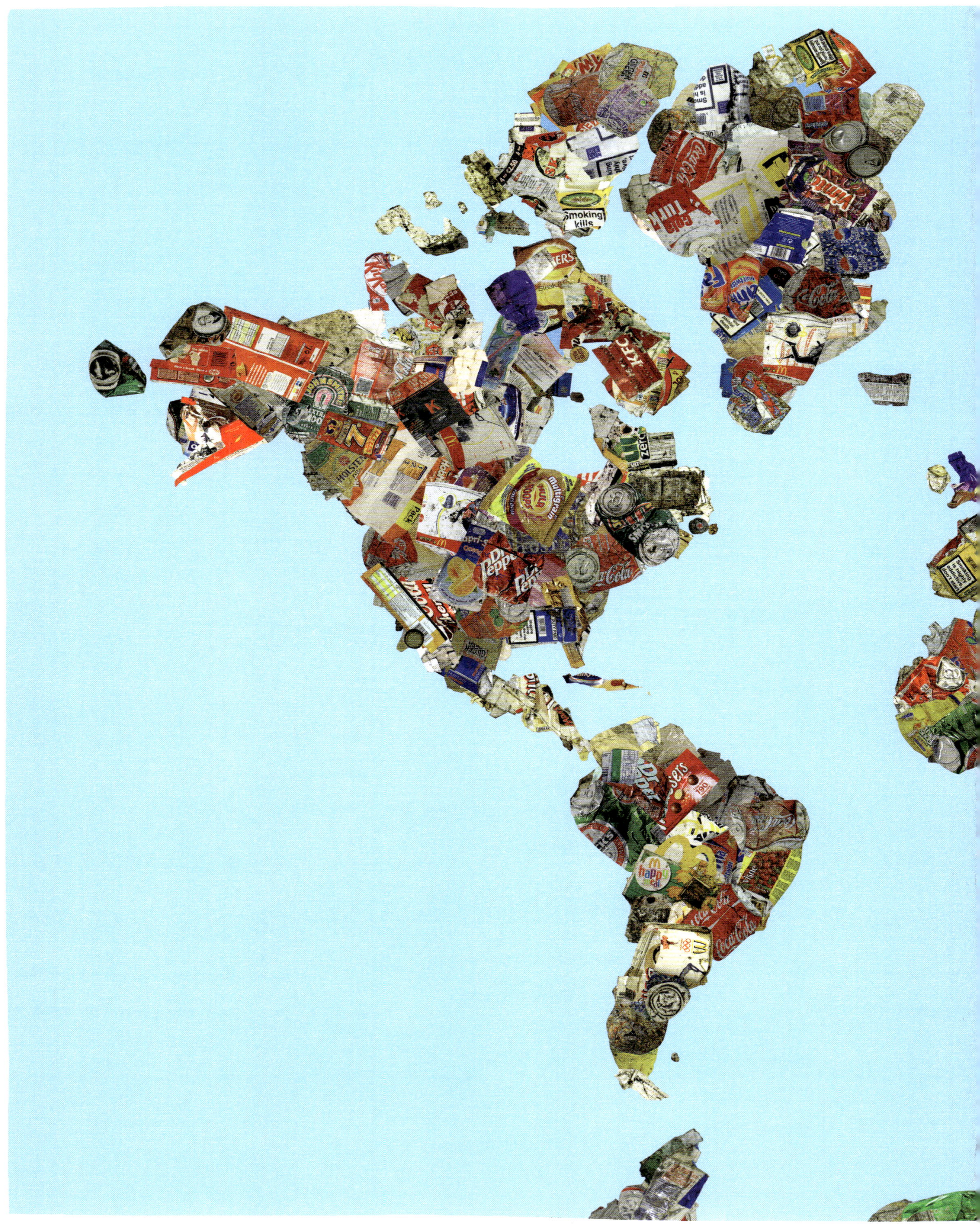

The world he portrays is completely choked with garbage
– even the deserts, mountains, lakes and ice caps are
covered. Is he commenting on pollution and the evils
of consumerism? 'I didn't intend to; I'm not trying to be
didactic, but the map obviously touches on global issues
such as our effect on the planet and the consequences
of manufacturing. Junked cars, for instance, are crushed
with all the upholstery and plastics inside before being
sent to China for recycling, where it has to be burned off.
And then we complain about their carbon emissions!

'Tapestries remind me of castles and the aristocracy;
so I'm dealing in opposites – using the highest form of
craft to elevate the status of rubbish and thereby raise
questions about value. Companies spend millions of
pounds on developing a brand name and logo and on
packaging – the packaging is often more expensive than
the product. So when a can is chucked away and gets
run over, what is it worth and whose responsibility is it?'
As a sculptor, Turk is best known for bronze casts
of bin liners filled with rubbish and for waxworks of
himself posing as Sid Vicious, Che Guevara, a tramp and
Marat, the French revolutionary.[2] The sculptures have
all involved collaborating with skilled craftsmen so, for
him, designing the tapestry was not a new experience.
'I'm comfortable with people making things for me',
says Turk. 'It's mainly a matter of pragmatism; I've been
involved in making most of the waxworks, but I get the
black bin bags cast in the foundry. I want things to be
made by the person best qualified and, in many cases,
that's me. But I wouldn't know how to go about weaving
a tapestry.'

[1] Produced in 1989 by Afghan embroiderers, Boetti's world map is divided into
countries each filled with its national flag.
[2] The tableau was based on Jacques-Louis David's 1793 painting 'The Death of
Marat'.

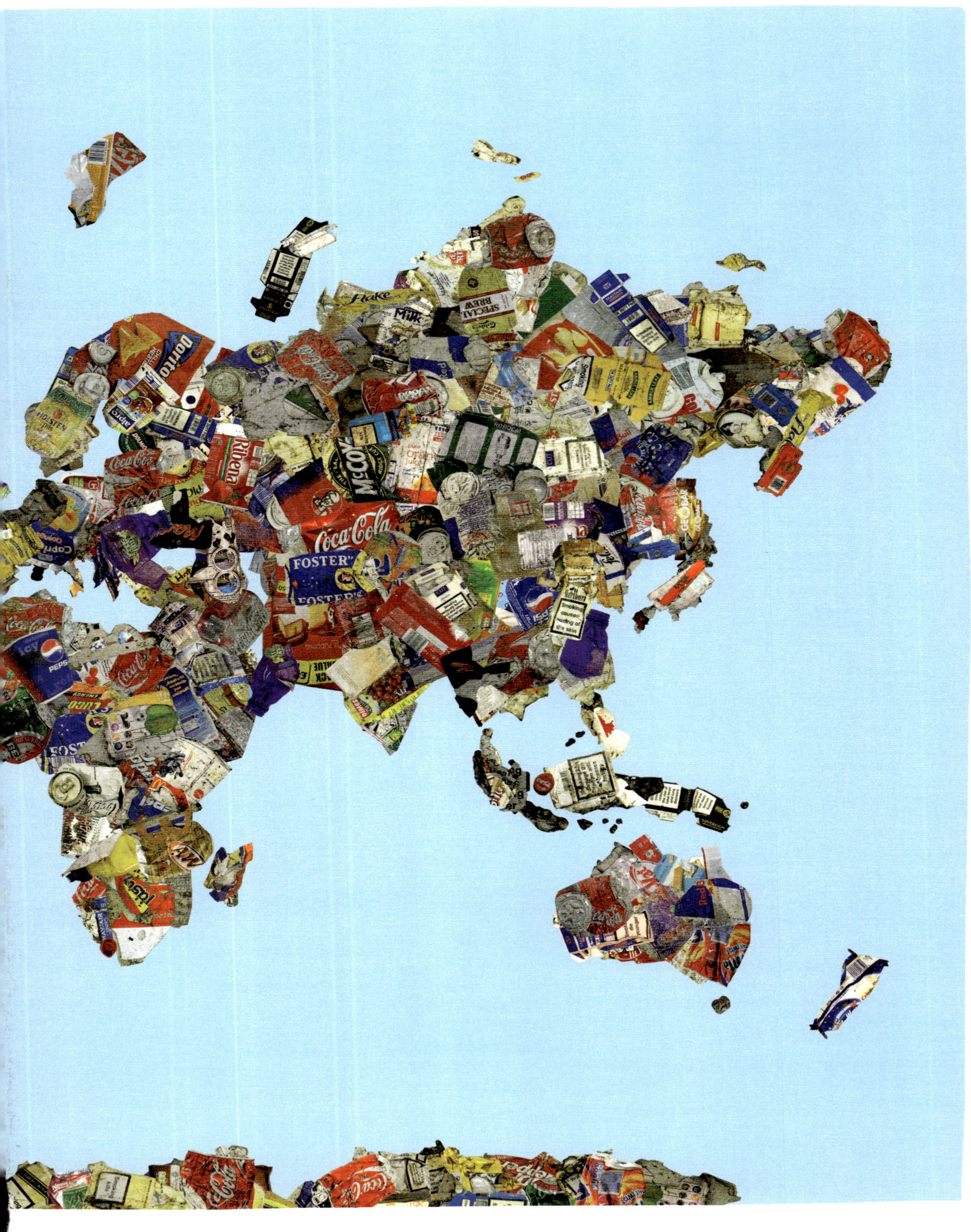

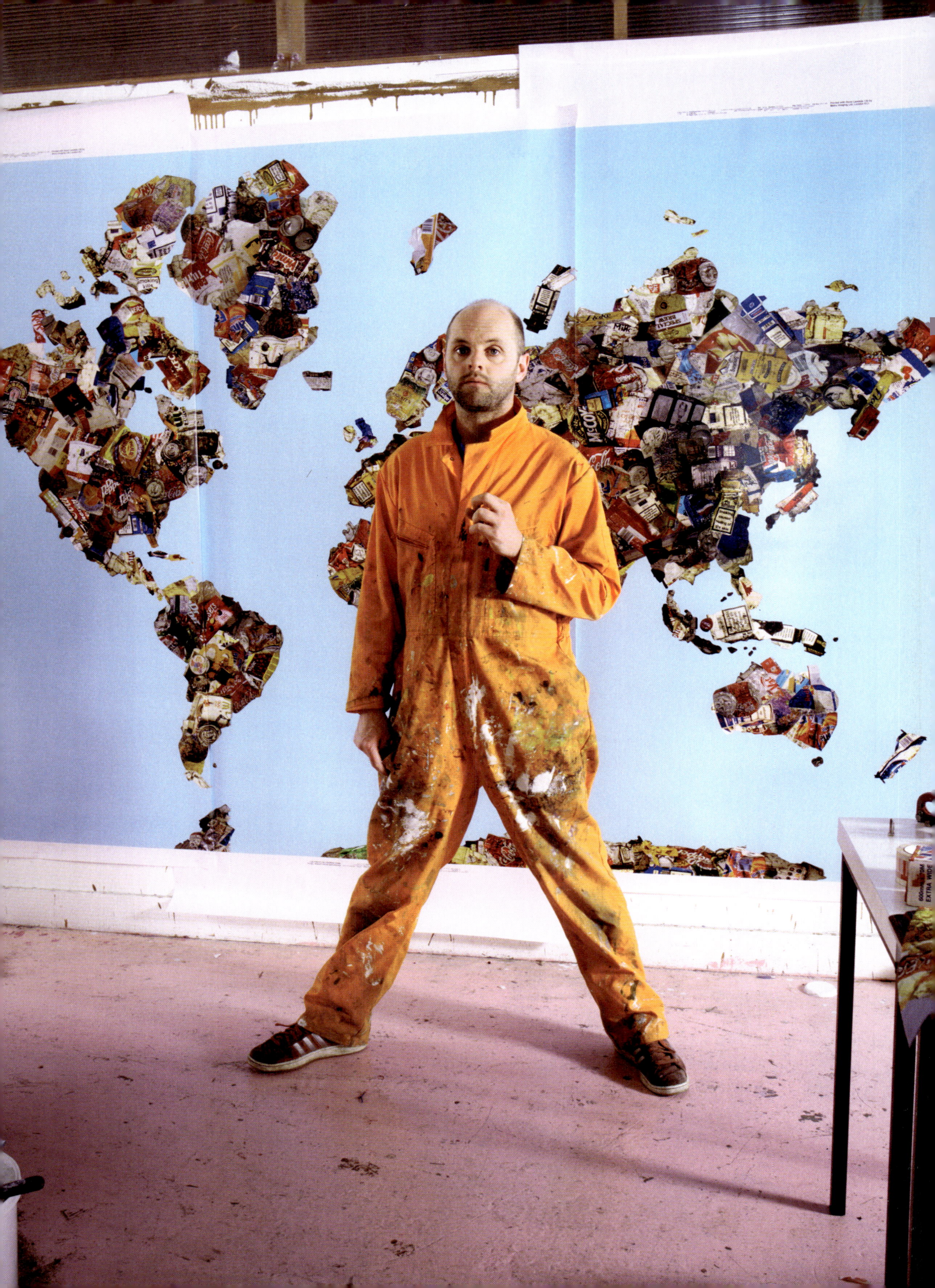

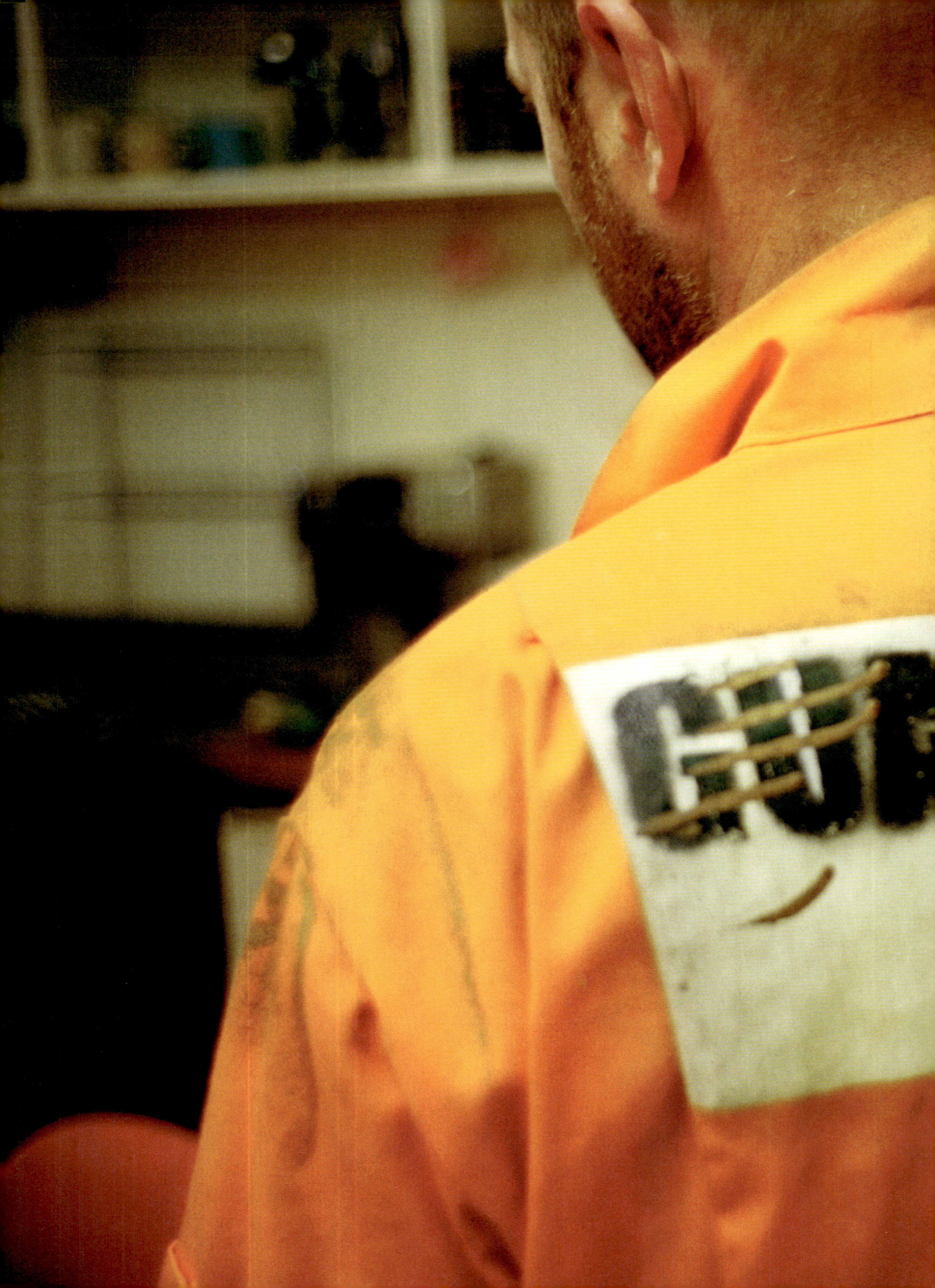

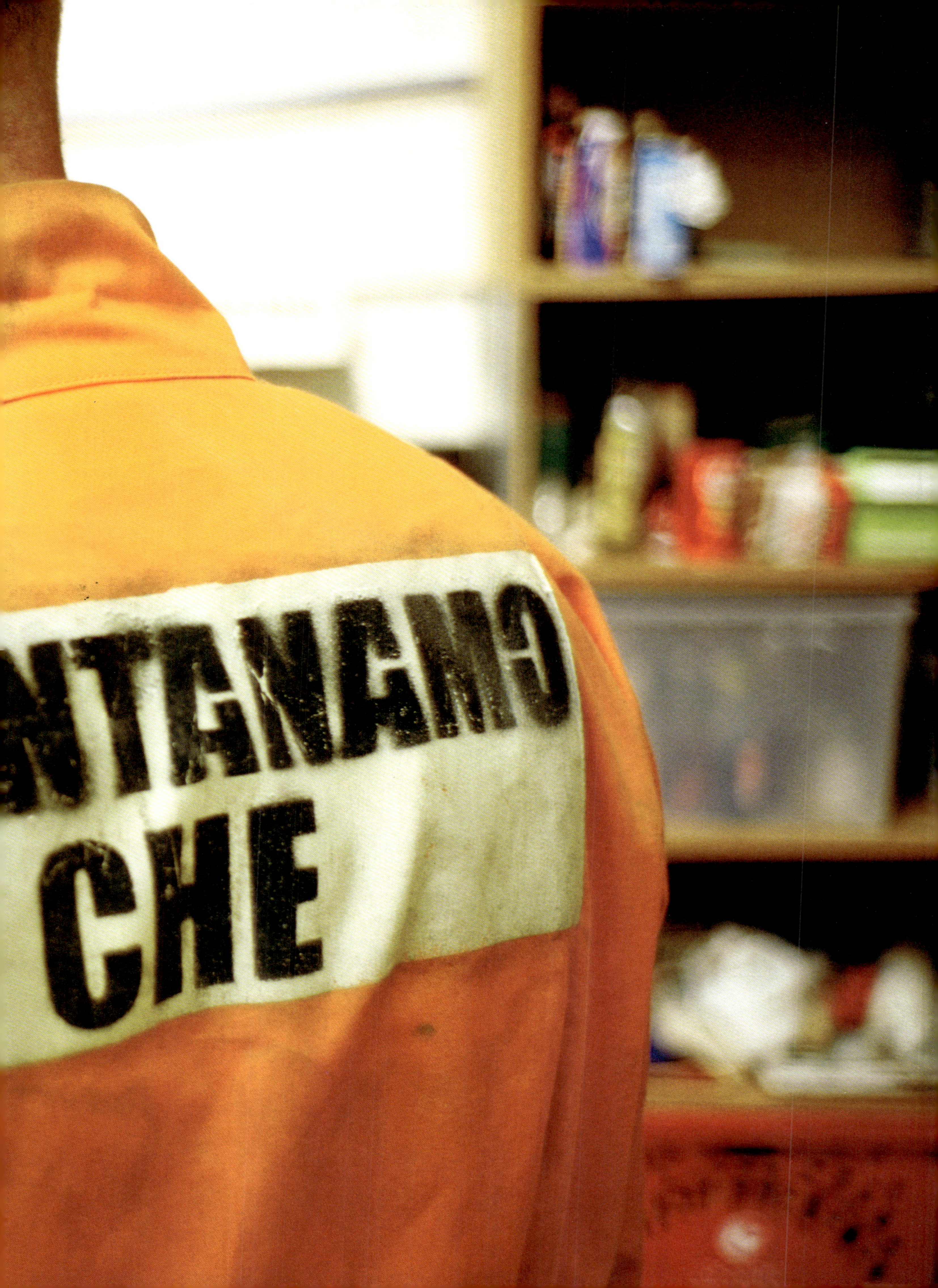

NTANAMO
CHE

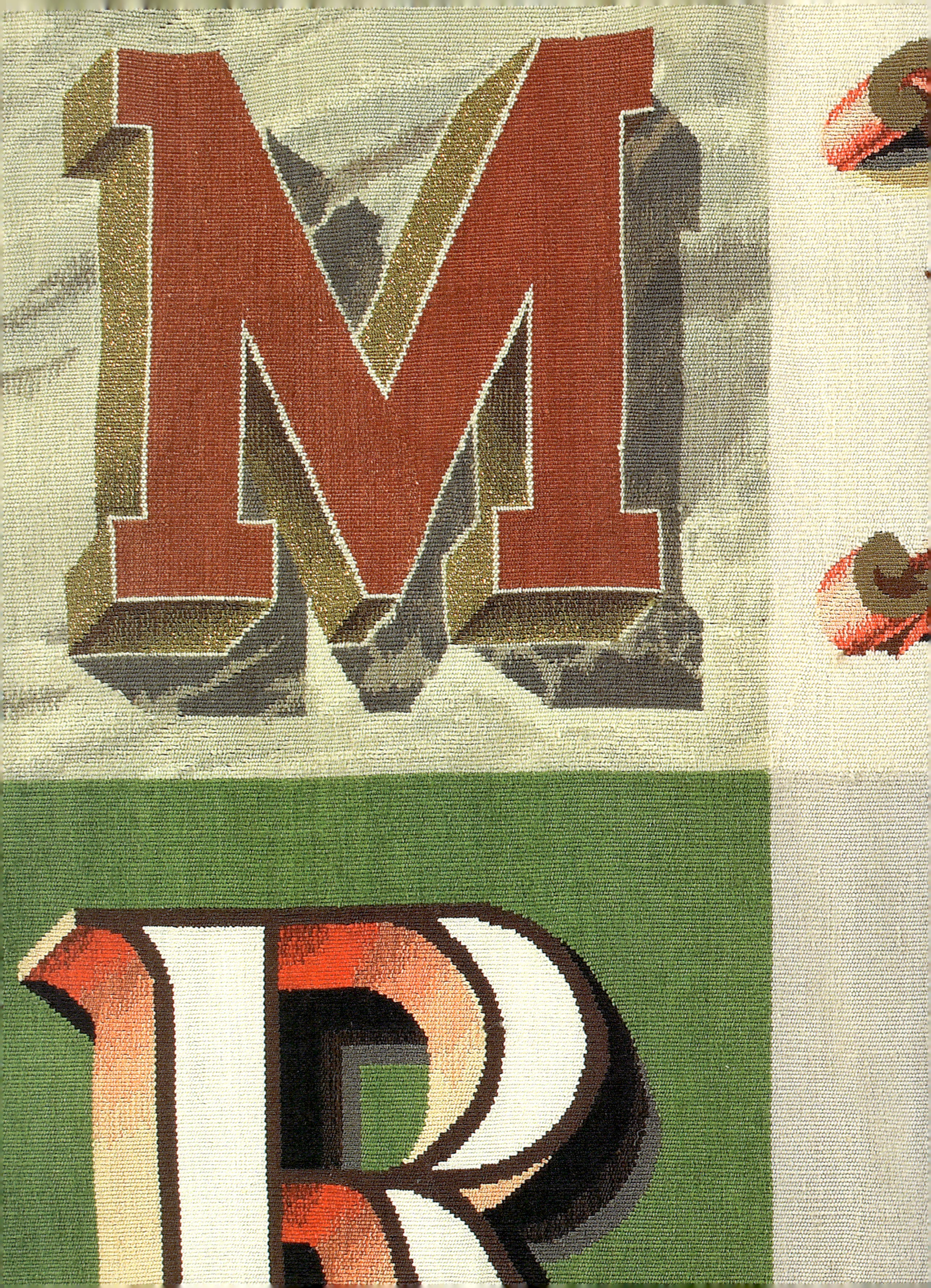

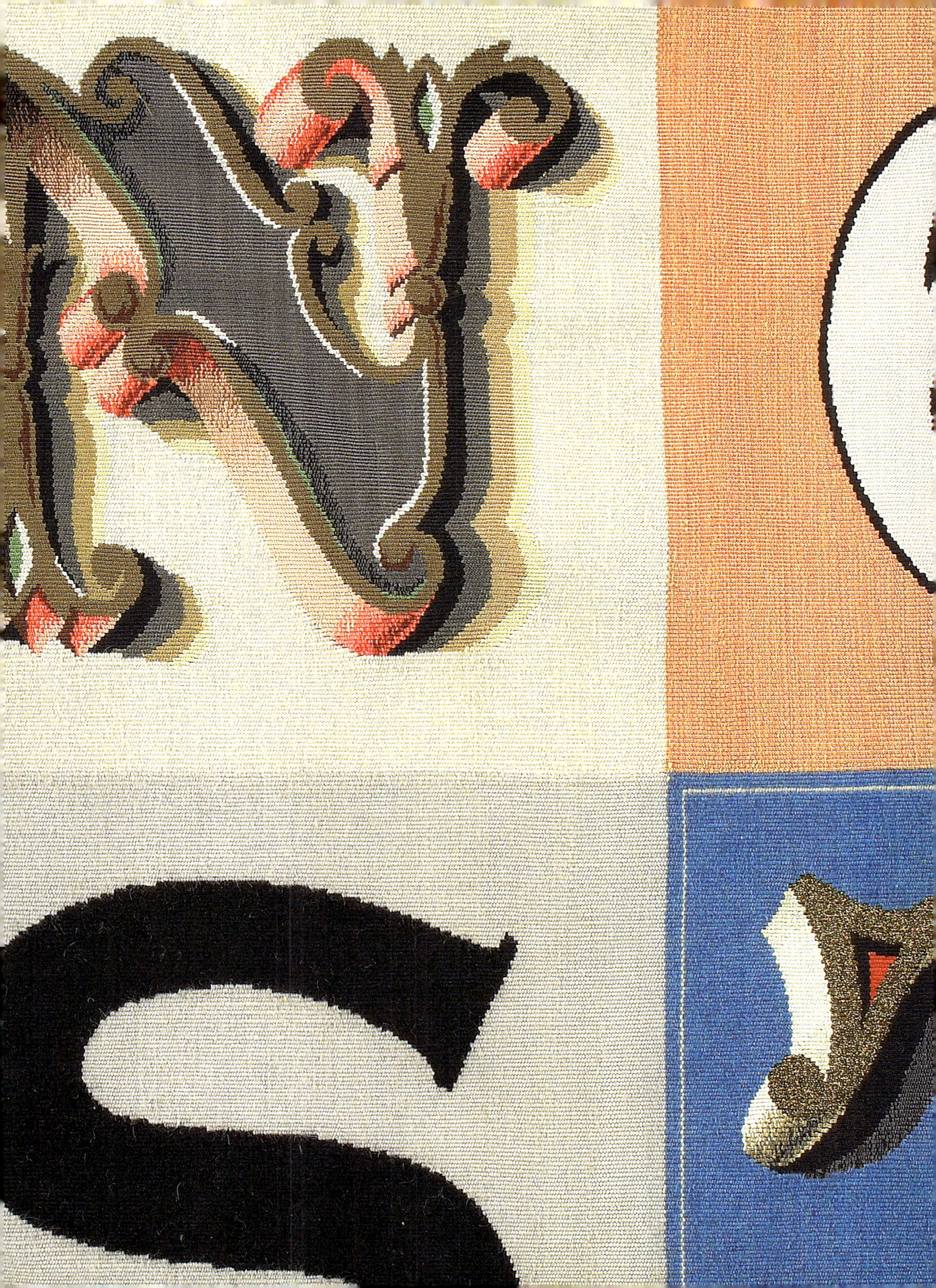

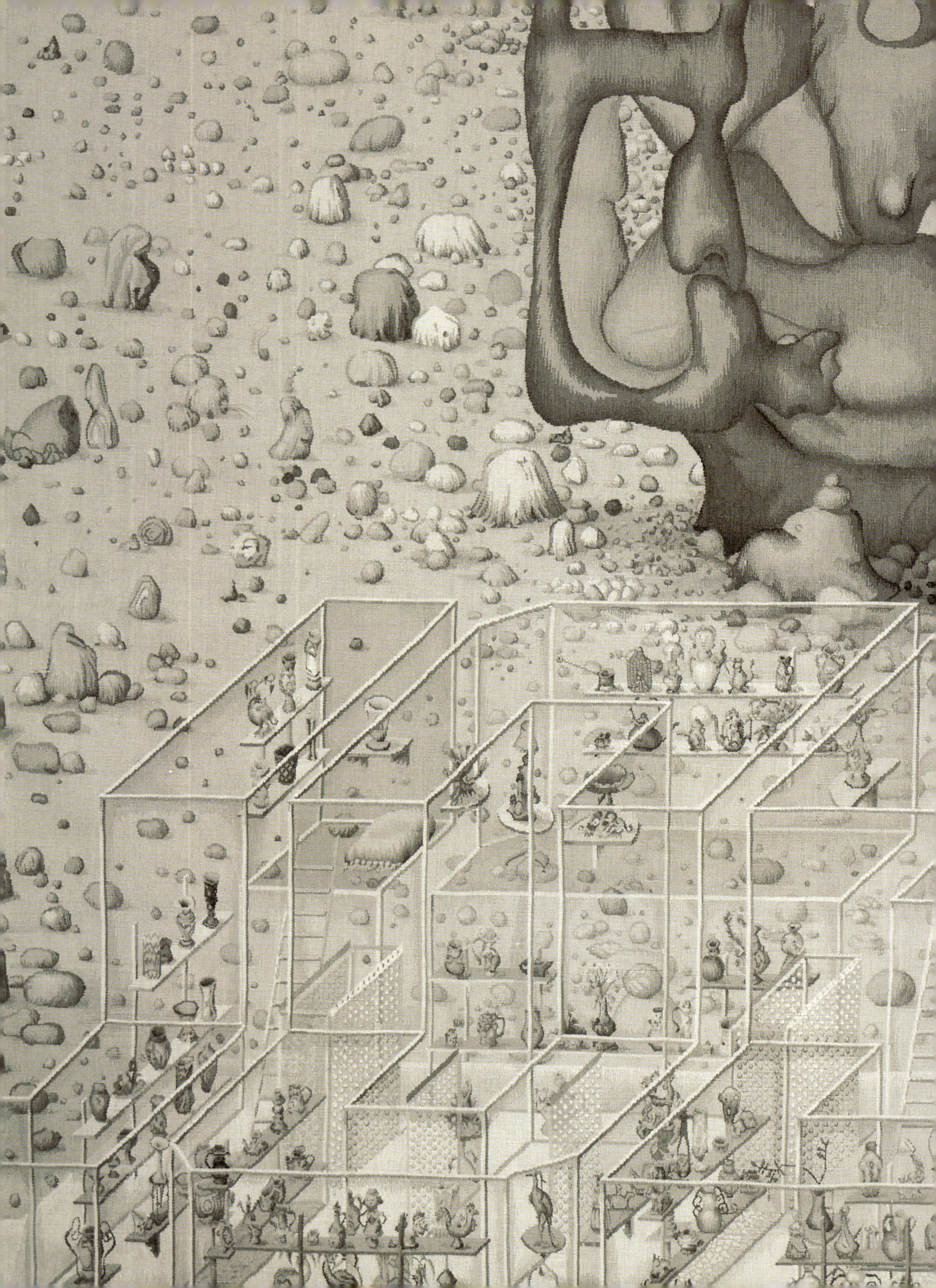

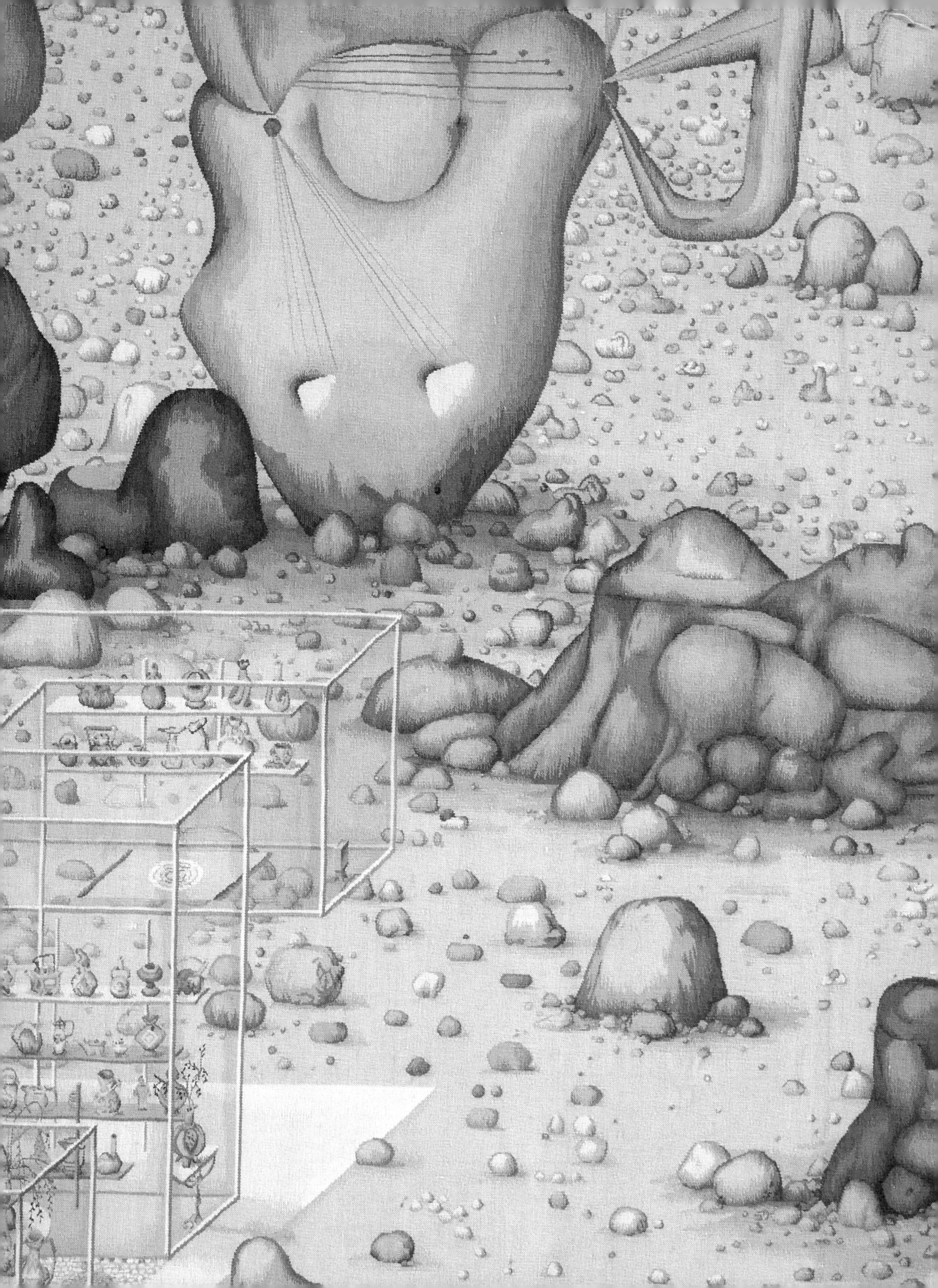

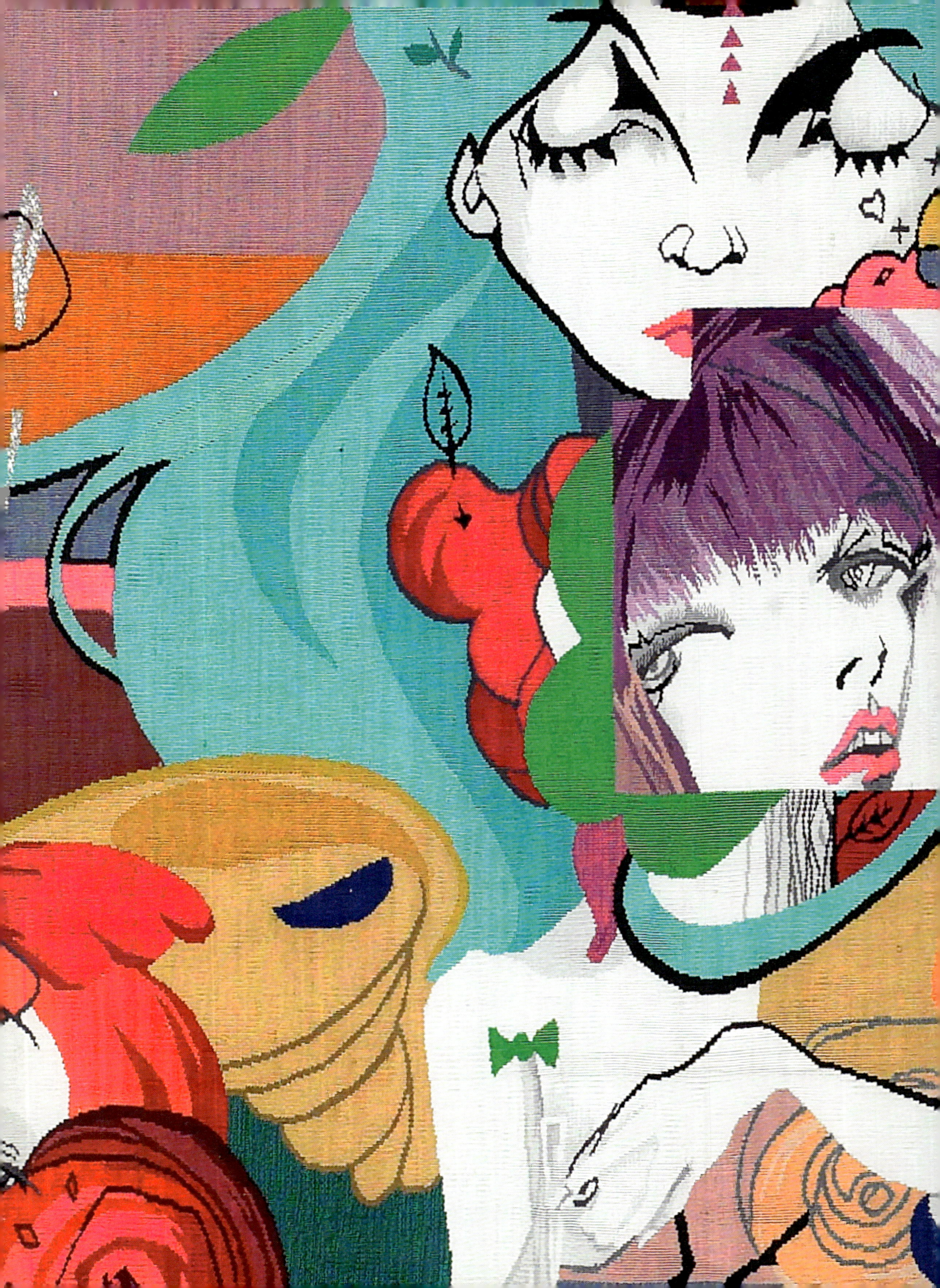

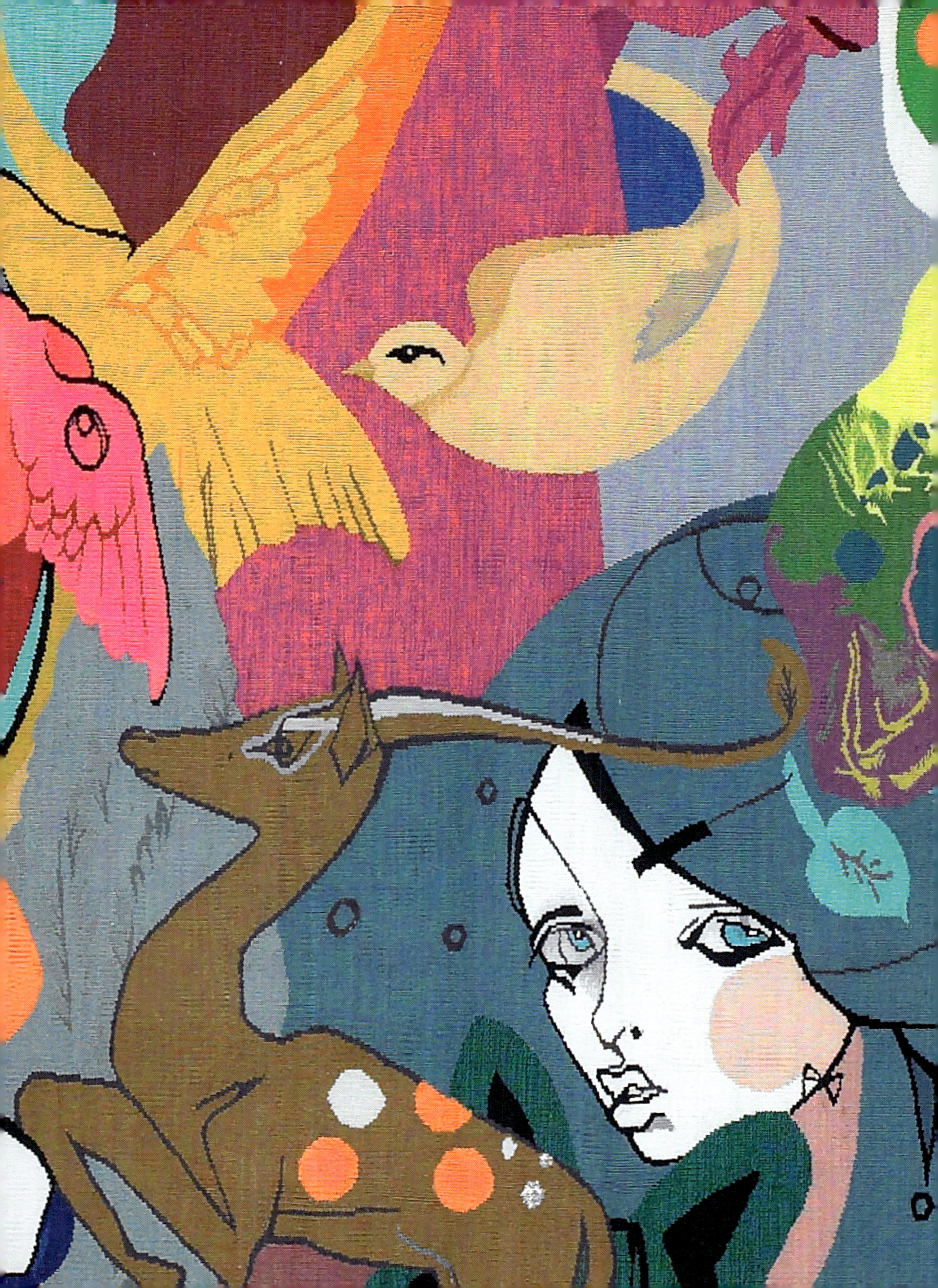

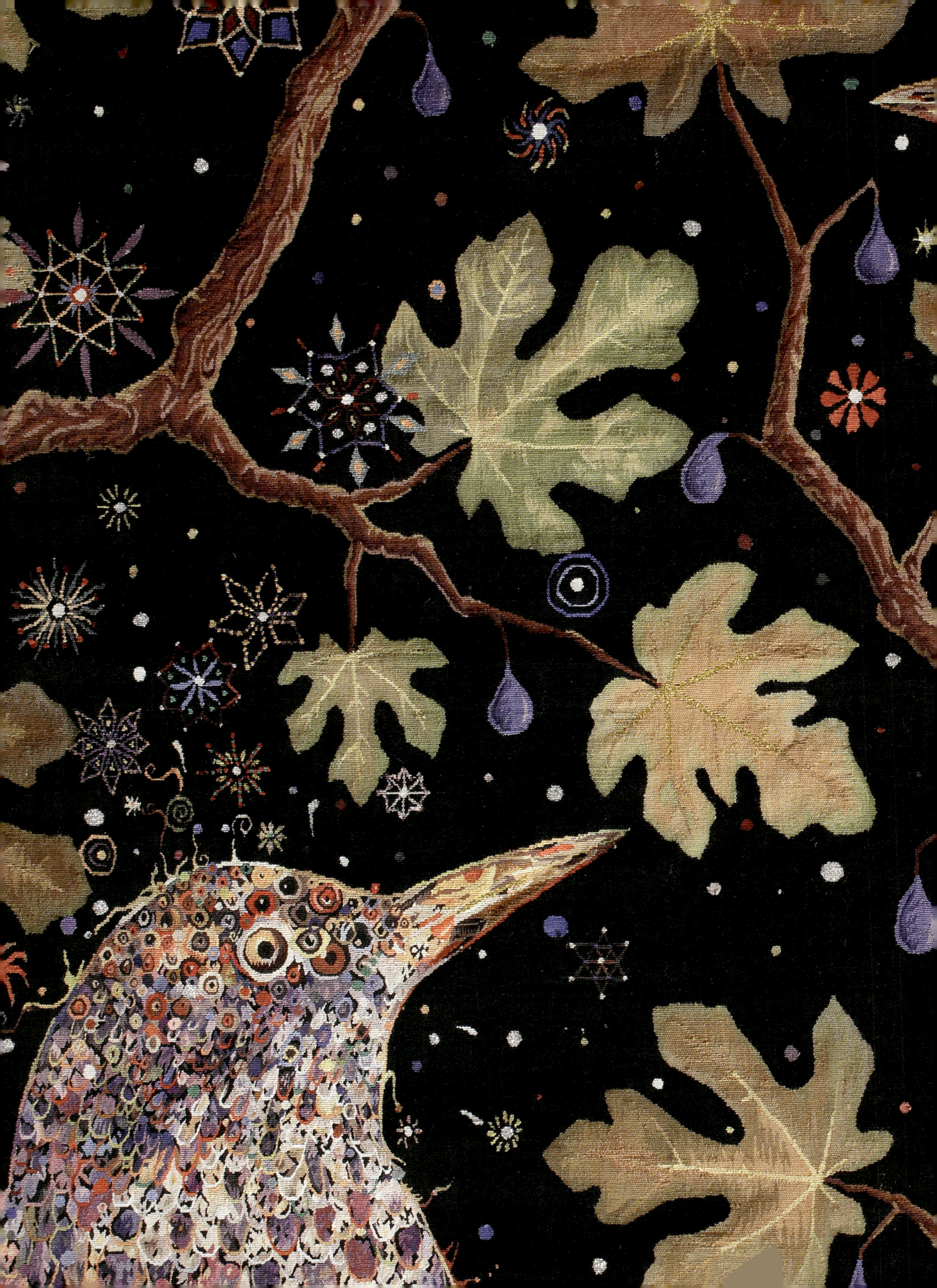

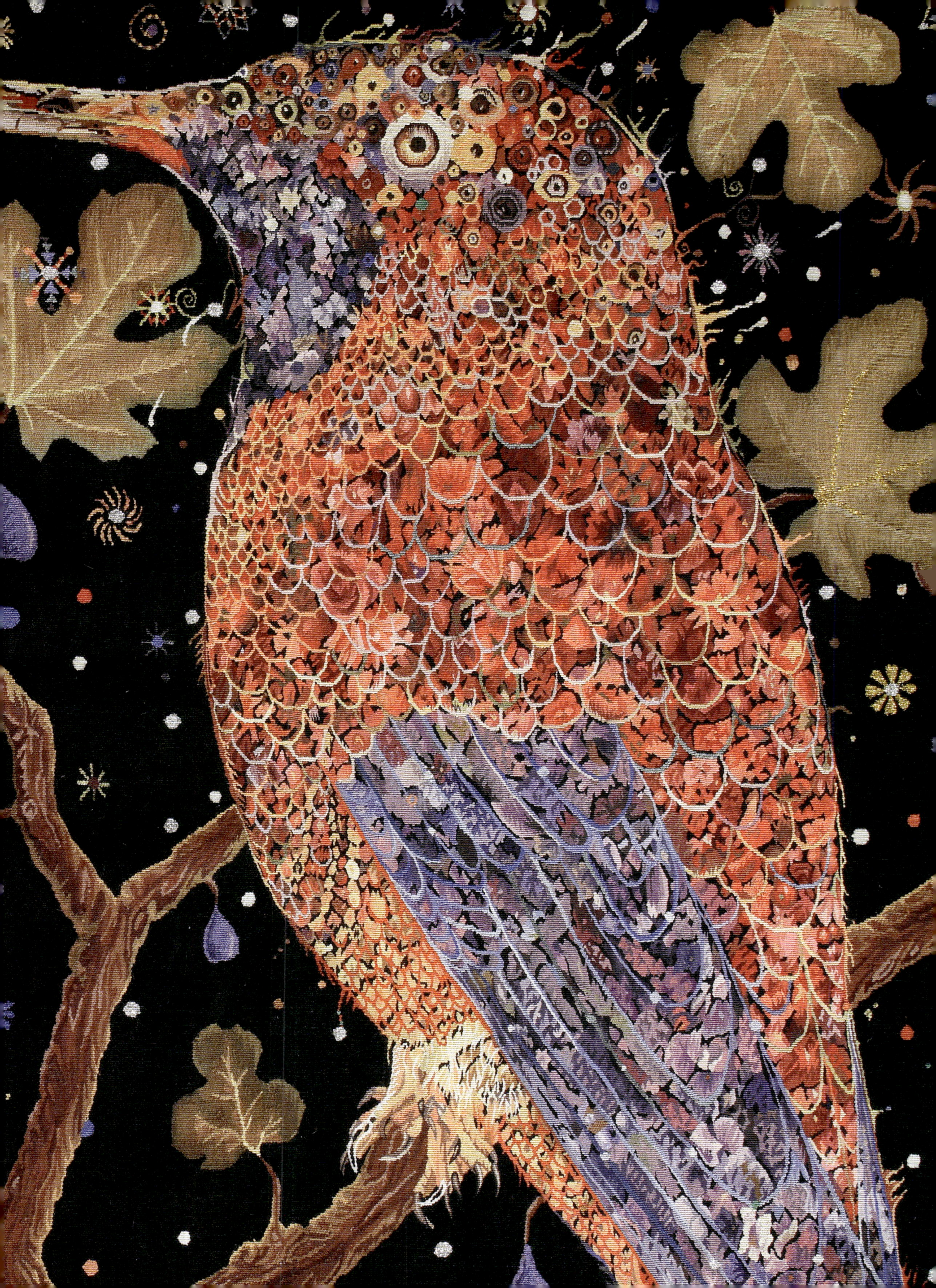

Georgie and Orchids
Gary Hume

'Georgie and Orchids' is based on one of a group of
pictures known as the 'Water Paintings', which Gary
Hume showed in the Venice Biennale in 1999 when he
was chosen to represent Britain. Three, sepia-coloured
line drawings of his naked wife are superimposed over
one another. The figures appear transparent, as though
drawn on separate sheets of acetate through which
one can see the pale cream ground. But the picture is
highly ambiguous since the background can also be seen
as flesh, and the women as solid substance. Several
dangling orchid fronds further complicate the picture by
adding another layer to the shallow space.

Hume has famously said: 'The surface is all you get
of me'[1] and, using enamel paint on aluminium, he has
produced a lustrous finish – impersonal, but immaculate.
But these are the very qualities that a tapestry can't
possibly achieve. Woven thread can't hope to mimic
the sleek rigidity of aluminium or the smooth sheen
of enamel paint; the oatmeal ground looks more like
raw canvas than metal and, ranging in tone from black,
through mid-brown to pale coffee, the outlines of the
women resemble melted chocolate. Embroidered over
the top in various shades of green silk, the foliage
catches the light and shimmers seductively. It may be
quite different from the painting but, nevertheless, the
tapestry is extremely beautiful.

'It's difficult to make a good looking tapestry from my
work,' Hume tells me. 'I'm using very little of what
tapestry is beautiful at, because I don't paint like that;
tapestry loves gradations and loathes a straight line. I
recently visited Henry Moore's barn at Much Hadam
and saw the tapestries there based on his drawings and
watercolours.[2] They are really fantastic; I wish I could
paint like that!'

Why didn't he design something specially for the project?
'I love tapestries, but all my work is unsuitable', he
explains. 'I would have had to do a whole new oeuvre.
I've made a tapestry once before based on a line painting

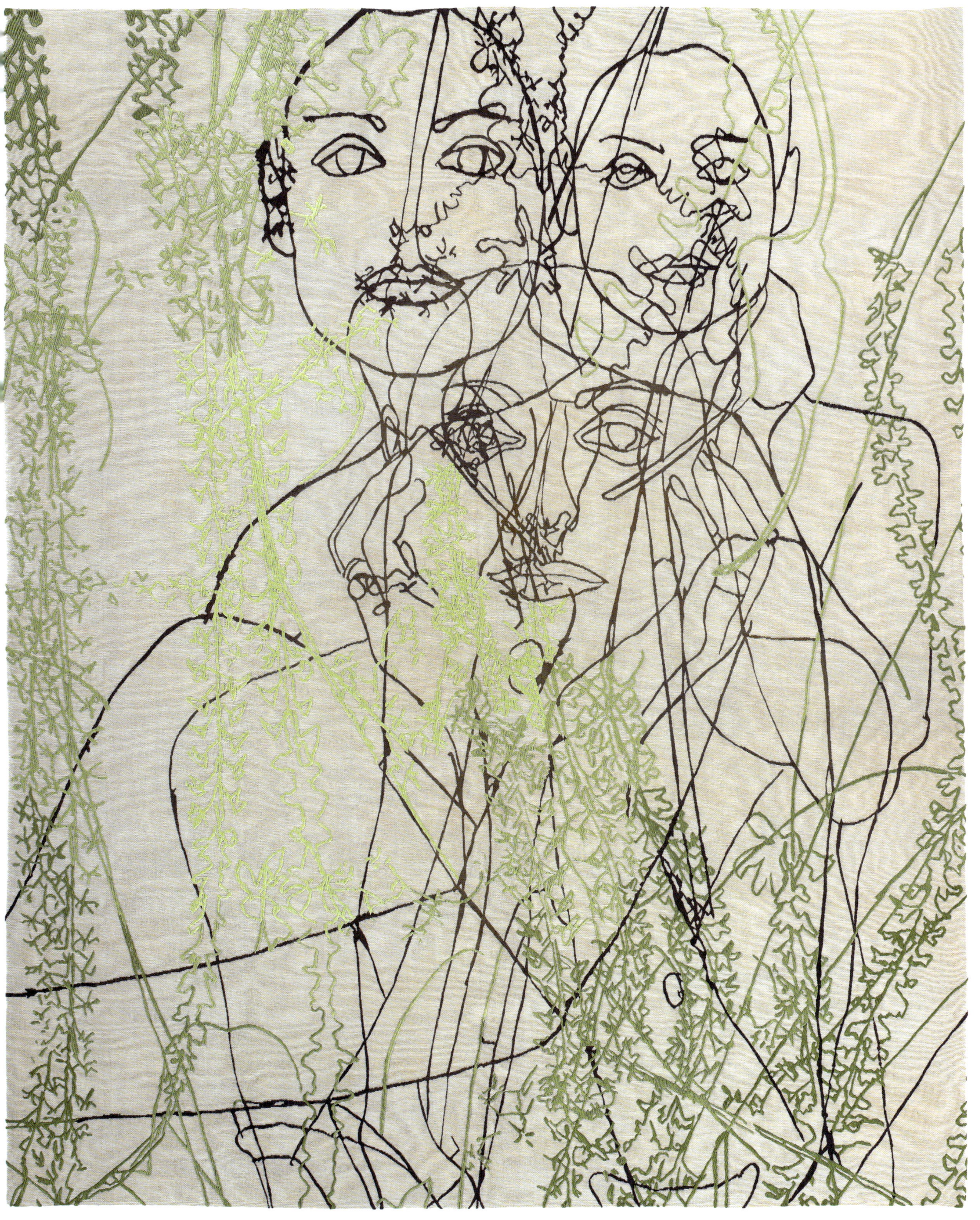

of a nude called 'Pauline' and I learned a bit from that; it half worked. I've also made a series of 'Garden Paintings' based on 'The Lady and The Unicorn' tapestries.[3] I like the flatness and the vertical hierarchy; there's very little pictorial space so everything is on top of each other.'

Although his work looks impersonal and non-expressive, Hume is very much a hands-on artist. 'Sometimes I can see the whole painting from the outset in my mind's eye', he has said of the process. 'But more often than not... I have to go with what the painting says to me. The painting is always informing me. I'm its servant; it's not mine. I'm doing what it wants.'[4]

How, then, does he respond to the fact that the tapestry was made by craftspeople a long way away? 'I'm a stranger to it because another hand was involved in the decision-making process; I can't tell what it's like, because I'm a virgin viewer. I'm also concerned about how you show it. How do you hang it on the wall without making it look like soft furnishings? When you see the tapestries at the V&A these questions don't arise, partly because you are thinking about the palaces where they were originally shown. Tapestries inhabit a very strange world. It's an incredibly old fashioned, time consuming medium that relates to mediaeval grandeur. They were hugely expensive draught excluders!

'But what's the purpose of making this translation, now? Does it alter something when you change a work from one medium to another? Chuck Close's tapestries are fantastic – they look just like the original photographs – but what's the point of them?[5] What makes a good tapestry over a strange one? Most tapestries are allegorical and they have action in them. Paul Noble creates a world in the same kind of way, so maybe the medium will reinforce his work, but I create pictures without a narrative so, in my case, it raises questions because the image looks weird. If I do another one, I'll try to answer some of these questions and maybe I'll follow your suggestion and make an image specially.'

[1] Quoted by Adrian Searle in 'Shut that Door', *Frieze* Summer 1993.
[2] Ten tapestries, woven by the West Dean Tapestry Workshop between 1976 and 1986, are on display in the Aisled Barn at the Henry Moore Foundation.
[3] 'The Lady and The Unicorn' cycle consists of six mediaeval tapestries titled 'Love', 'Hearing', 'Sight', 'Touch', 'Smell' and 'Taste'. They feature a lady, lion and unicorn in an exquisite formal garden and are in the collection of the National Museum of the Middle Ages, Paris.
[4] Quoted by Paul Vallely in *The Independent* 8.9.2007.
[5] Based on daguerreotypes of his friends, Chuck Close's tapestries were shown at the White Cube Gallery, London in October 1977.

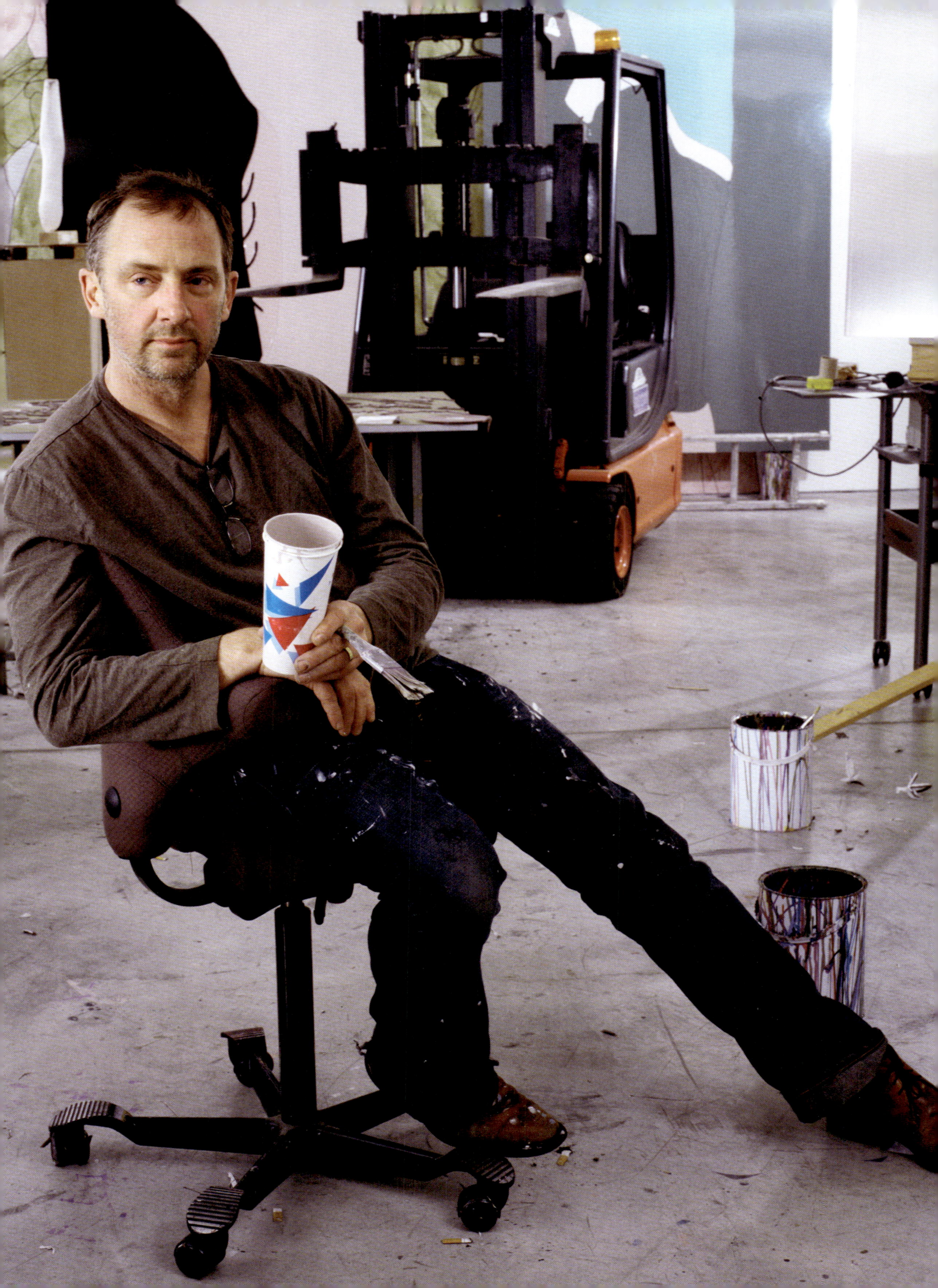

Far from the Madding Crowd
Julie Verhoeven

Julie Verhoeven made her name as a fashion designer
and illustrator, but is increasingly interested in making
drawings for their own sake. Her design features
trademark girls, whom she describes as swinging
'between sweetheart pretty pretty and angst-ridden
desperate.'[1] They appear in the company of doves and
animals such as a rabbit, toad, cat and deer that could
have leapt straight from a Disney cartoon. 'They're not
inspired by Disney, so much as Snoopy from the *Peanuts*
cartoon and the *Miffy* children's books, done in beautiful
flat colours. Everyone loves animals, but the driving force
is the female. I resisted doing bodies, so I cut them off at
the head, making them more dreamy.'

Two hands holding a heraldic sword and a pink unicorn
add a mythic dimension to the gathering. 'I remember
myths and fairy stories from childhood, but I don't look at
them now and can't bear nostalgia. Fantasy has a sickly
slant to it – sugary, which I don't like. Everything I like is
much darker, but I looked at 'The Lady and the Unicorn'
cycle of Mediaeval tapestries in Paris.'[2]

Columns, pedestals, trees and flowers suggest a garden.
'I don't really like nature', she says. 'I'm more interested
in architectural elements; I'm not big on foliage and I
have a real aversion to parks, but I love drawing columns.
The design was done in stages. Initially it was for an
individual piece, but then I was included in this project
and panicked because it was no longer a commercial
tapestry but an art work. The design was far too ordered,
so I tried to make it more random by collaging on pools
of enamel paint, which upset the whole thing and look a
bit psychedelic – as though everything is dissolving.'

The texture is the same throughout the tapestry, but
areas of shading in the women's faces and hair have
been captured with amazing subtlety. Translated by
the weavers into dense clusters of finely modulated
stitching, the swirls of liquid colour are the most beautiful
areas. 'I've designed textiles', says Verhoeven, 'but I was
stunned that the tapestry is so true to the original.'

Far from the Madding Crowd
2.75 x 2.05m (9ft x 6ft 10in)
Wool and silk tapestry, 2008

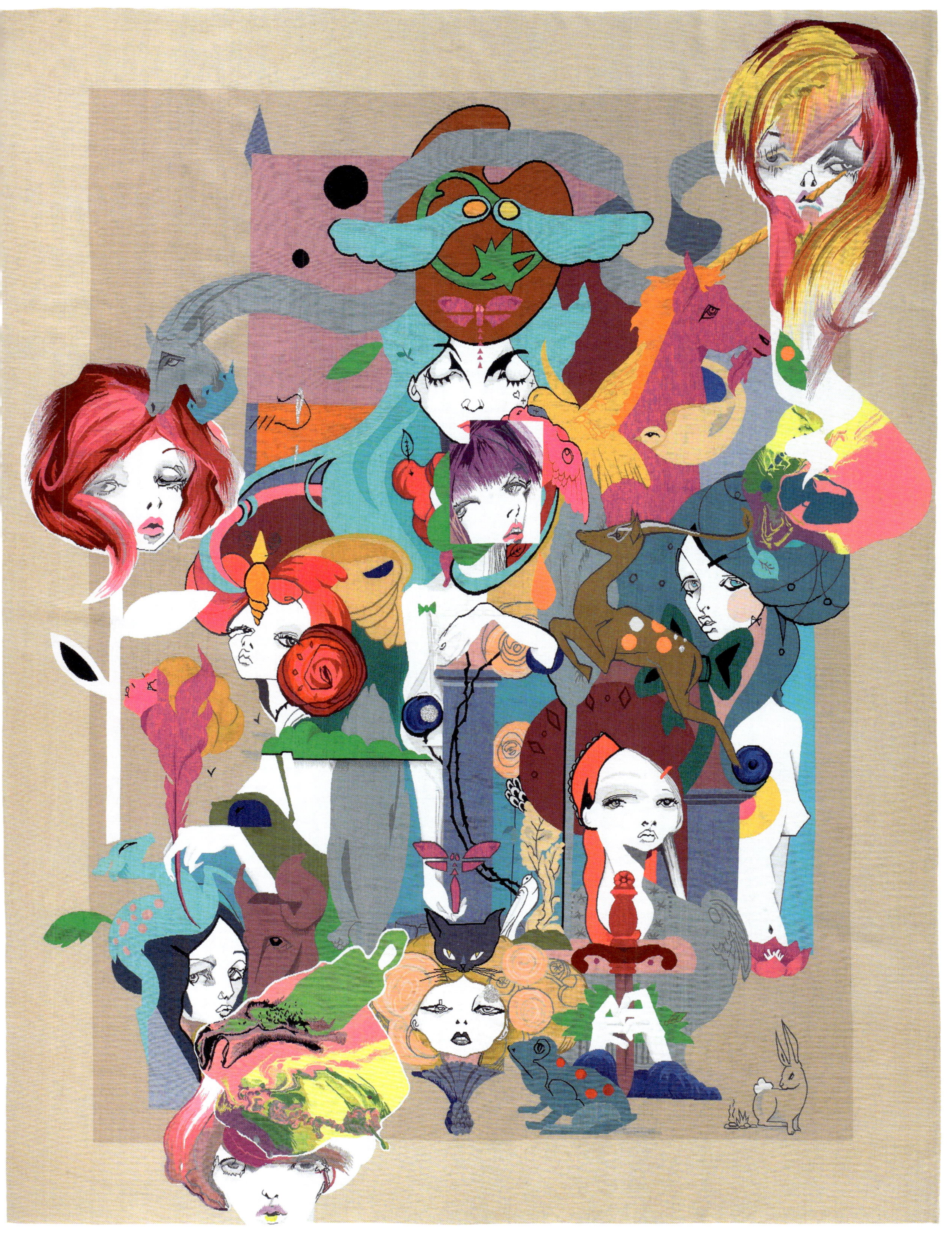

[1] Quoted in *IdN* Vol 14 No 3.
[2] 'The Lady and The Unicorn' cycle consists of six mediaeval tapestries titled 'Love', 'Hearing', 'Sight', 'Touch', 'Smell' and 'Taste'. They feature a lady, lion and unicorn in an exquisite formal garden and are in the collection of the National Museum of the Middle Ages, Paris.

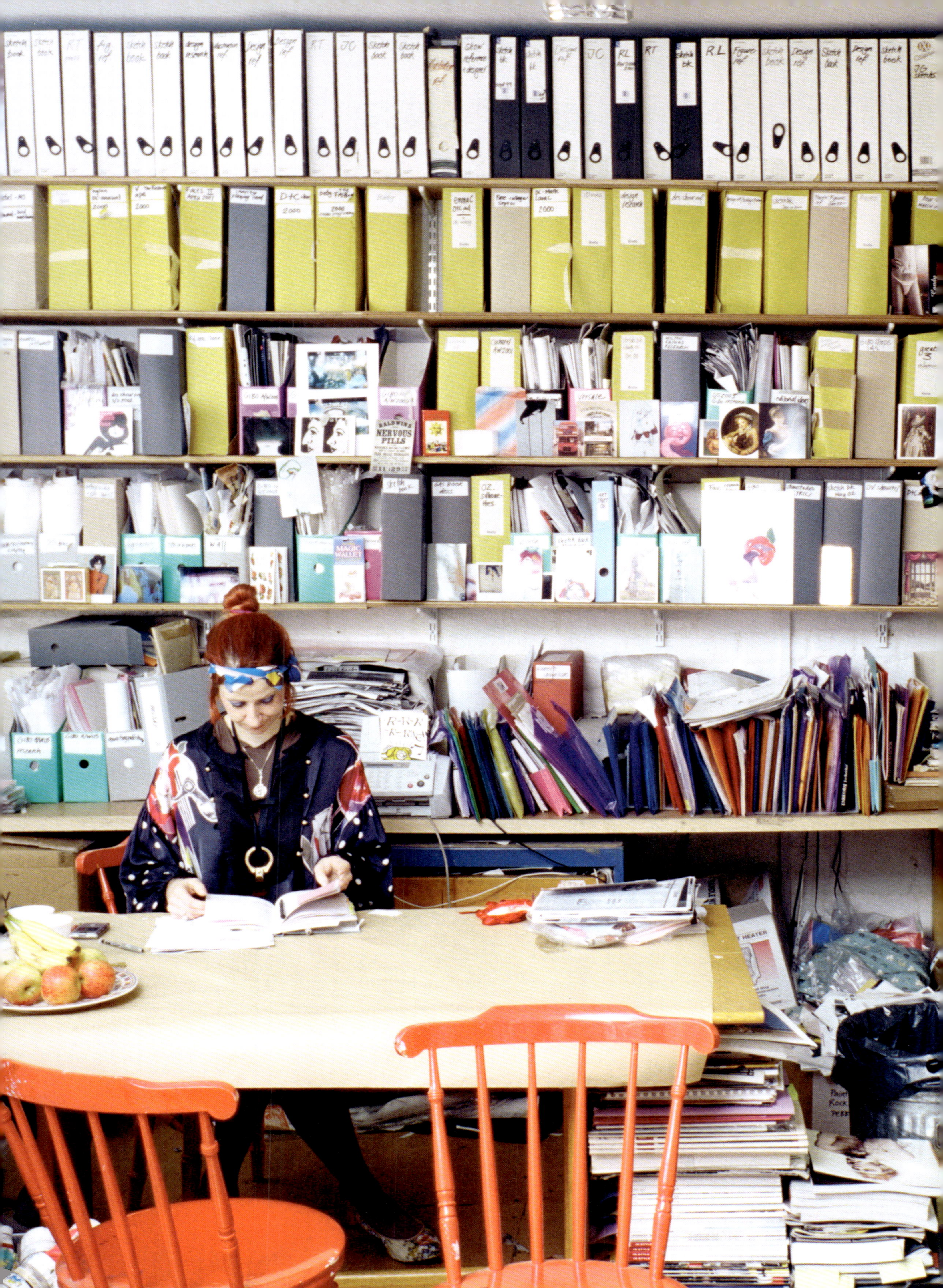

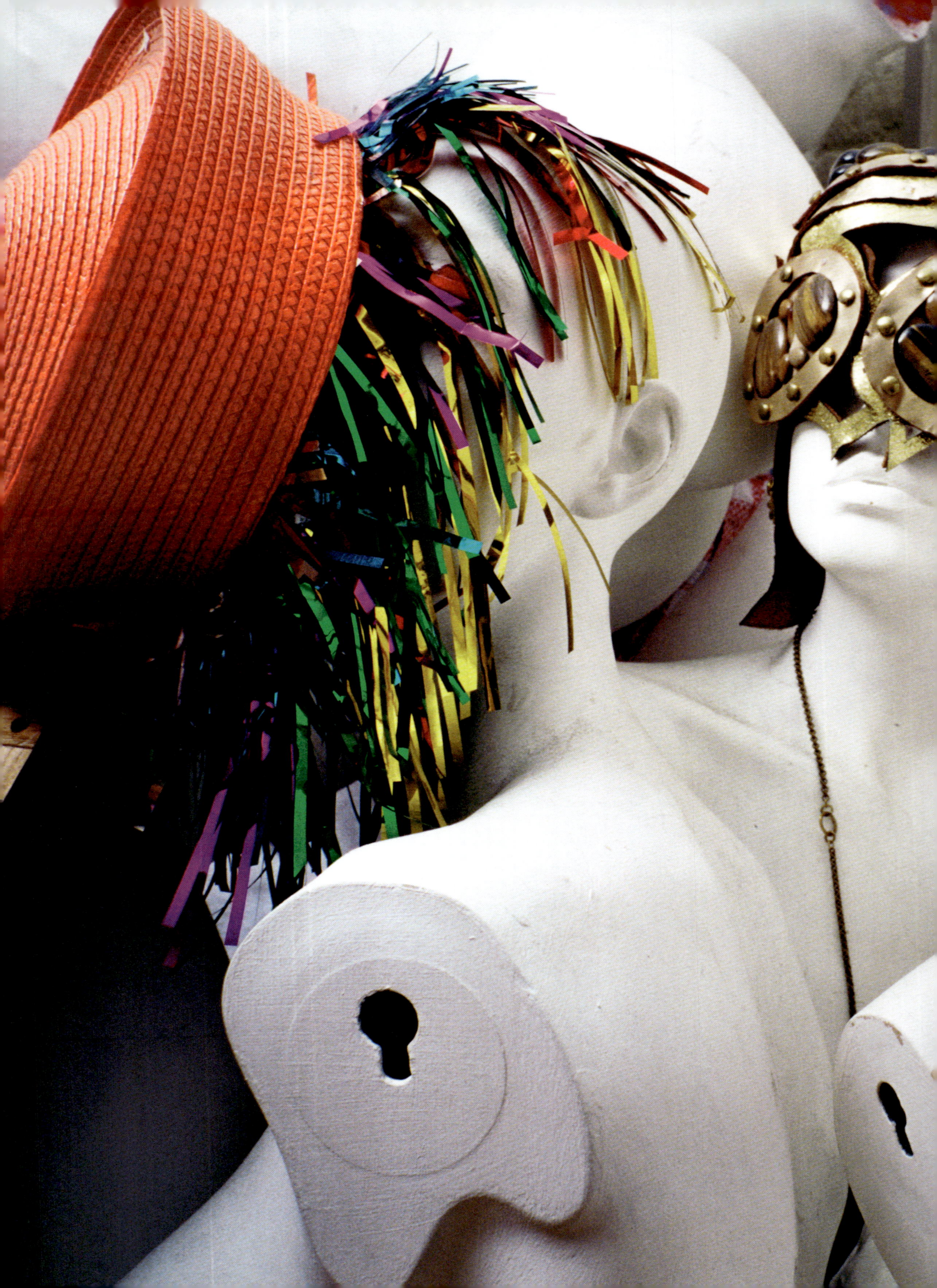

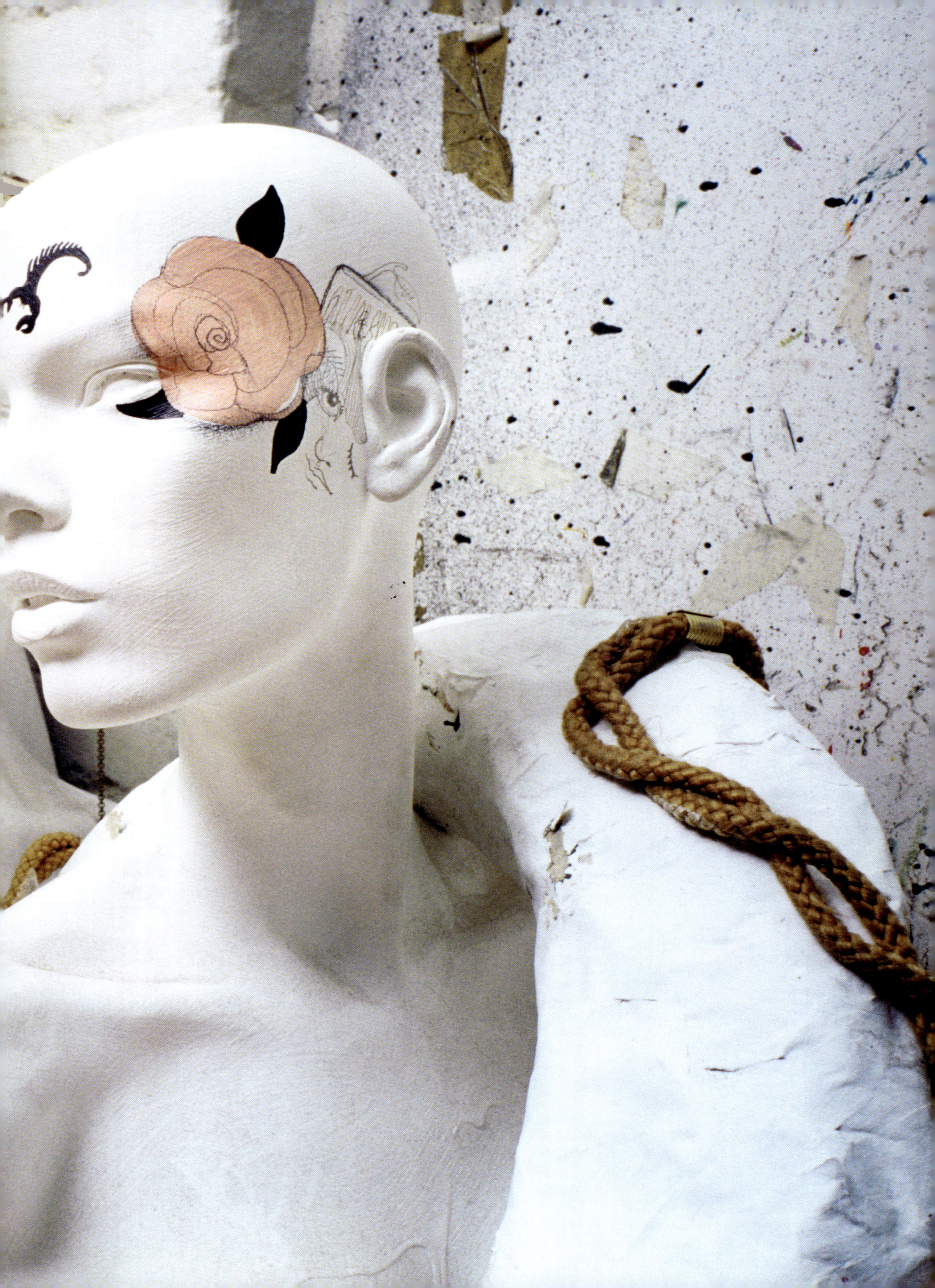

Jaime Gili

The shards of colour that slice through the space in Jaime Gili's paintings appear to be on the move. With their large scale and explosive force, these kinetic bursts of energy seem to be blasting their way into the future, while clearly referring to the past. It's as though they are propelling into the twenty-first century a message articulated nearly a hundred years ago by the Italian Futurists and pioneers of Russian abstraction, such as Mikhail Larionov and Liubov Popova. Gili is not a postmodernist, though, picking over the relics of failed belief systems. Far from being a requiem for misplaced optimism, his work embodies the euphoria of renewed conviction. The scale and vitality of his paintings is like a clarion call arousing people from the torpor of resignation or defeat.

Gili grew up in Caracas, the capital of Venezuela where, in the 1950s, international modernism flourished and artists and architects collaborated on buildings that exemplify the fusion between the arts envisaged by the pioneers of abstraction. By the time Gili began studying art in the late 1980s, though, developers were tearing the city apart and dismantling important buildings.

'There have been three moments of modernism in Venezuela', Gili tells me, 'in the fifties, the seventies and now. In the 1950s the right-wing dictator, Marcos Pérez Jiménez undertook big projects so that he would be remembered. He built the Central University in Caracas, for example.[1] Then Op Art was invented in Venezuela and, during the 1970s, a lot of public art projects were undertaken by artists like Jesús-Rafael Soto. Most have since fallen into disrepair, although some are being restored; you have to see how the light bounces off the work. Now Hugo Chavez is investing in infrastructure – building highways, a railway, new towns and so on– but it's not the same as in the fifties. His plan is to make South America strong against the U.S. So, in Venezuela, modernism is perceived as an unfinished project – something still to be achieved.'

Zelada
2.5 x 2.14m (8ft 2in x 7ft)
Wool, silk and artificial silk tapestry, 2008

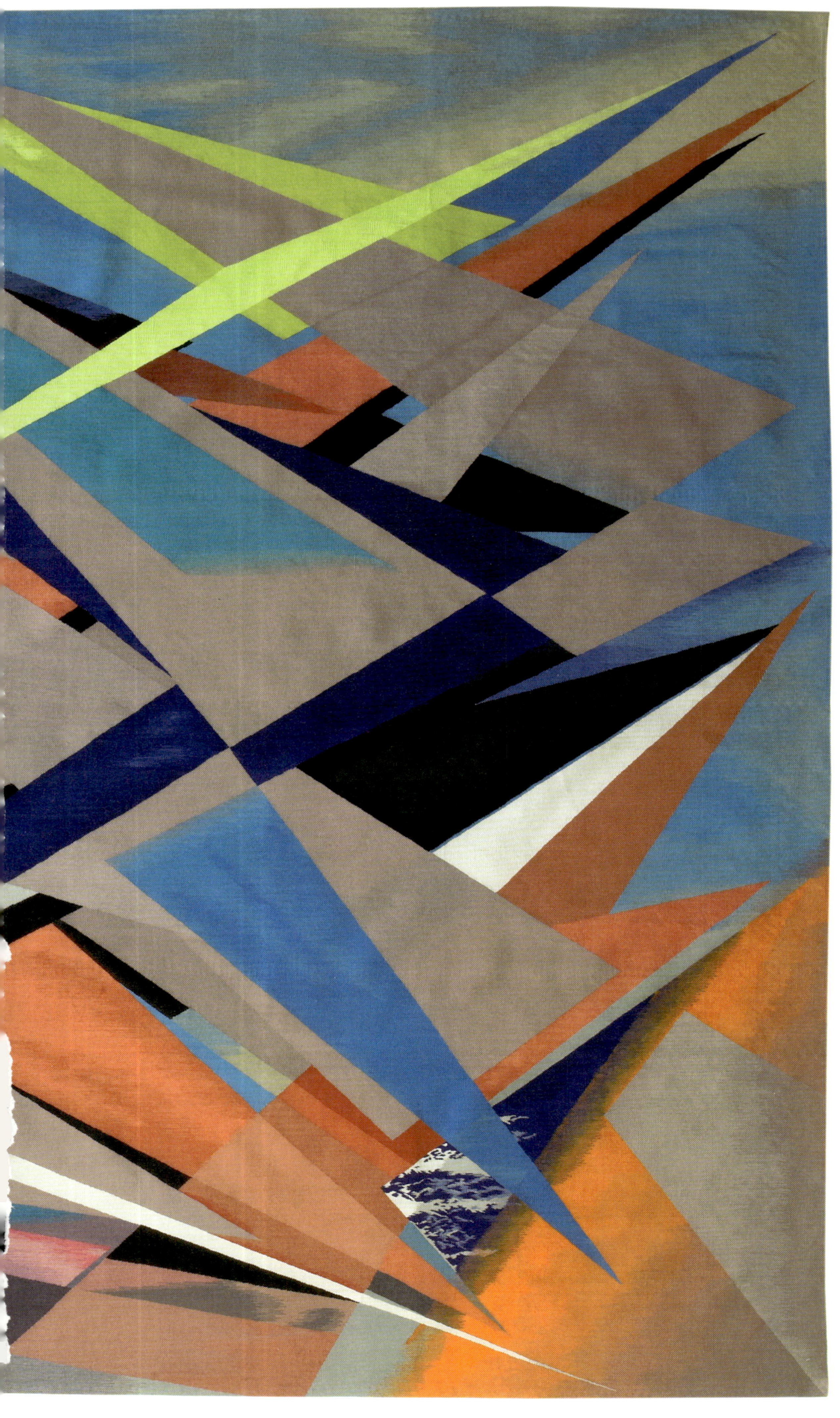

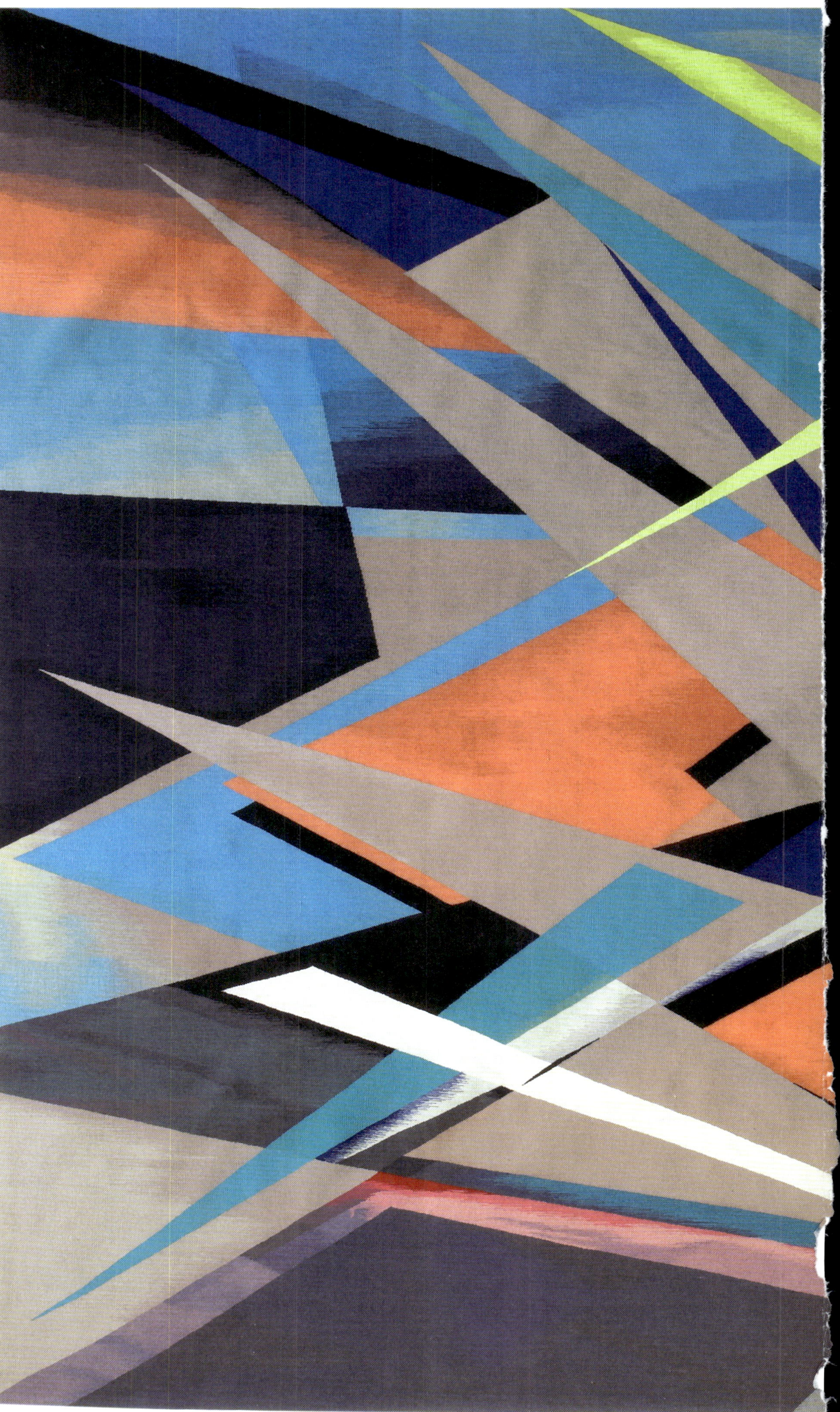

Why, then, did he go abroad to study? 'It's important
to have eyes that are trained outside', he explains,
'and then come back and adapt modernism so that
it becomes ours. It's necessary for us to have a local
tradition, so as not to feel like an offshoot of the United
States of America.'

Recently he has designed some stickers for the
motorcycle-taxi drivers who operate in Caracas. Attached
to their helmets and bikes, the patterns can be glimpsed
speeding around the city. 'Caracas is totally choked
with traffic', says Gili, 'so the bikes are vital as a way of
getting people around. For me the blocked city is like a
metaphor for the way modernism has ground to a halt in
Venezuela. We need to find a way to re-energise it.'

Does he think of himself as a Venezuelan artist? 'I'm
married to a Venezuelan woman and I come back here
a lot, though I still live in London. It's a good time to be
here at the moment, because oil prices are rocketing,
there is money around and people are spending it on art!'

The bike stickers seem far more appropriate as a
medium for his imagery than tapestry. The shapes in
his paintings read as splinters of glass, or beams of light
shooting across empty space; but, in the tapestry, they
coalesce into a web of interlocking planes. Instead of
light, air and movement, there is density and stasis.

Why was he interested in such an archaic medium;
did he design something specially? 'Painting is also an
archaic form!' says Gili. 'I had in mind the tapestries
that Goya made for the King of Spain. They are very
beautiful – much lighter in subject than his paintings.
Remembering Goya, I made a painting with the correct
proportions. A lot of decisions had to be made in terms
of translating it from one medium to another, though,
such as picking out the white and fluorescent areas in
silk so that they shimmer.'

His paintings are like an embodiment of speed – they zap

you in the face, as it were. Tapestry, on the other hand,
is slow; it takes a long time to visually unpick his design
– to fully appreciate its beauty, subtlety and complexity.
Gili often stands his paintings on the floor or places
them across a corner against a backdrop patterned with
shapes that conflict with those on the canvas to create
the visual equivalent of noise.

'The tapestry looks as if it should explode beyond the
edges like a star burst', agrees Gili. 'It would be nice to
install it around a corner or let it hang onto the floor. I did
a screenprint on fabric at the University of Essex and I
hung it from one corner or laid it on a table, folded. If I
could hang the tapestry in a similar way, I would.'

[1] Declared a World Heritage Site by UNESCO in 2000, the university was
designed by Carlos Raúl Villanueva, who invited artists like Fernand Léger, Jean
Arp and Victor Vasarely to contribute to the design; Alexander Calder designed
some ceiling mobiles that also perform an acoustic function.

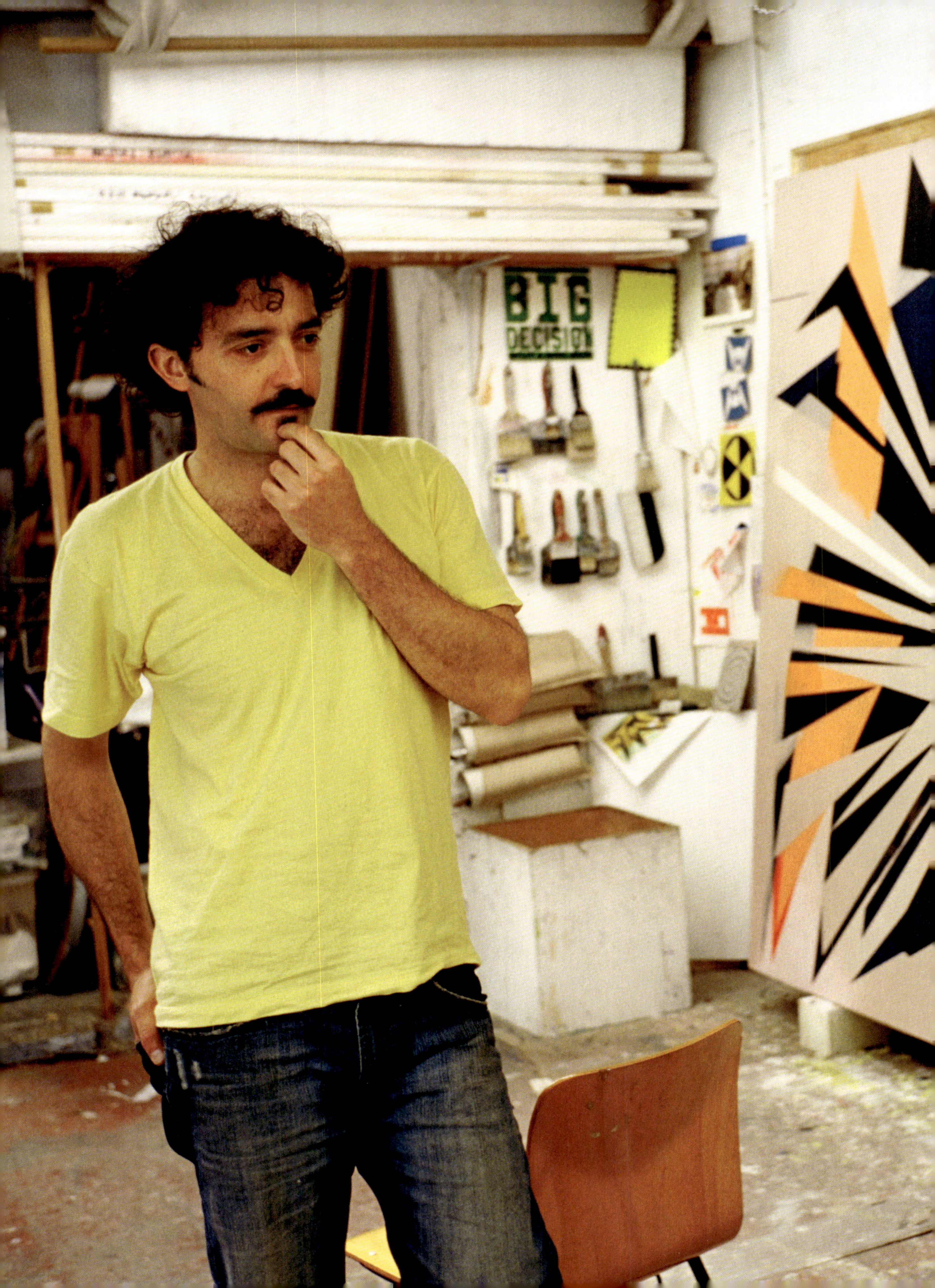

BIG
DECISION

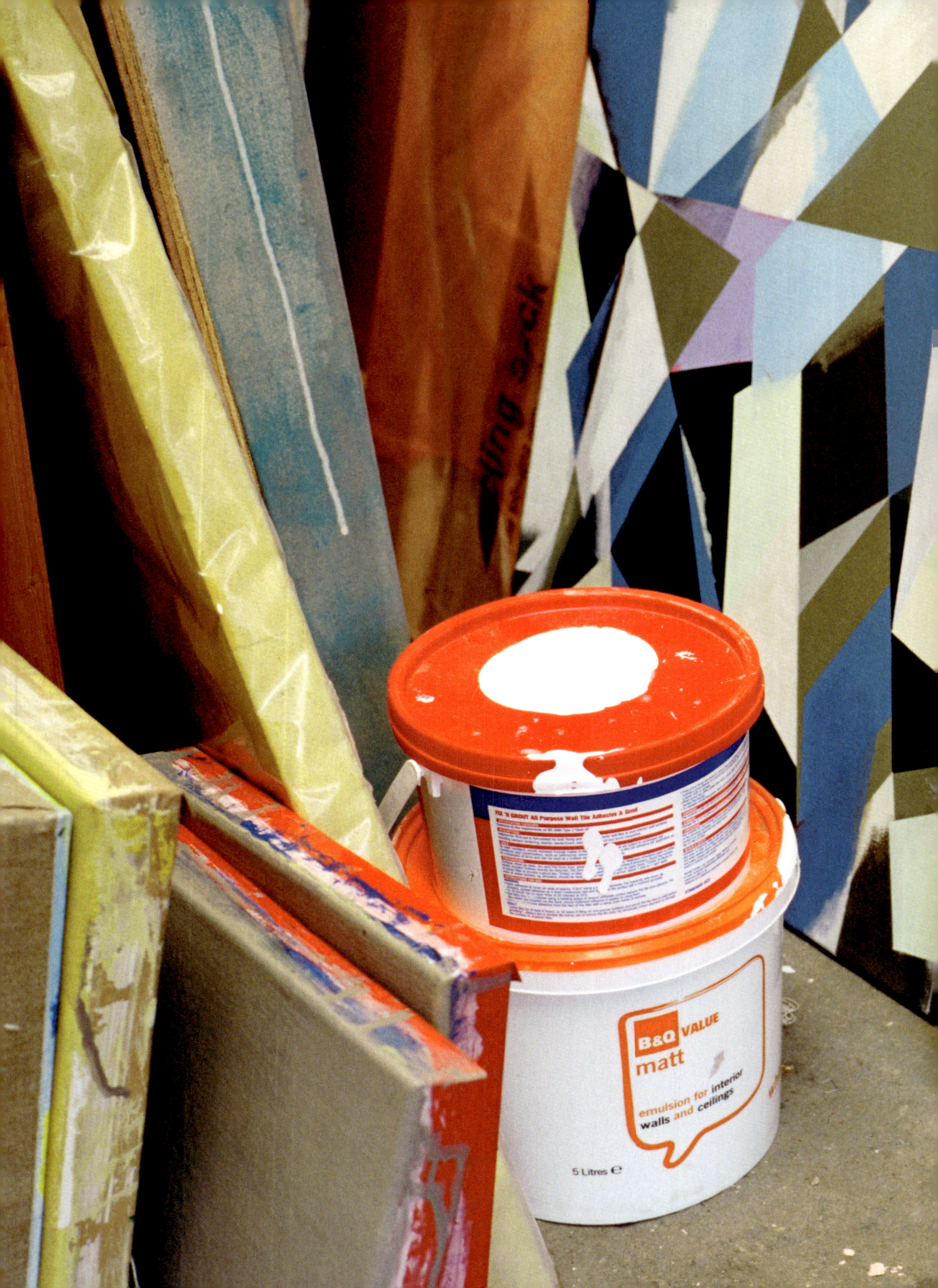
FIX 'n GROUT All Purpose Wall Tile Adhesive & Grout
B&Q VALUE
matt
emulsion for interior
walls and ceilings
5 Litres e

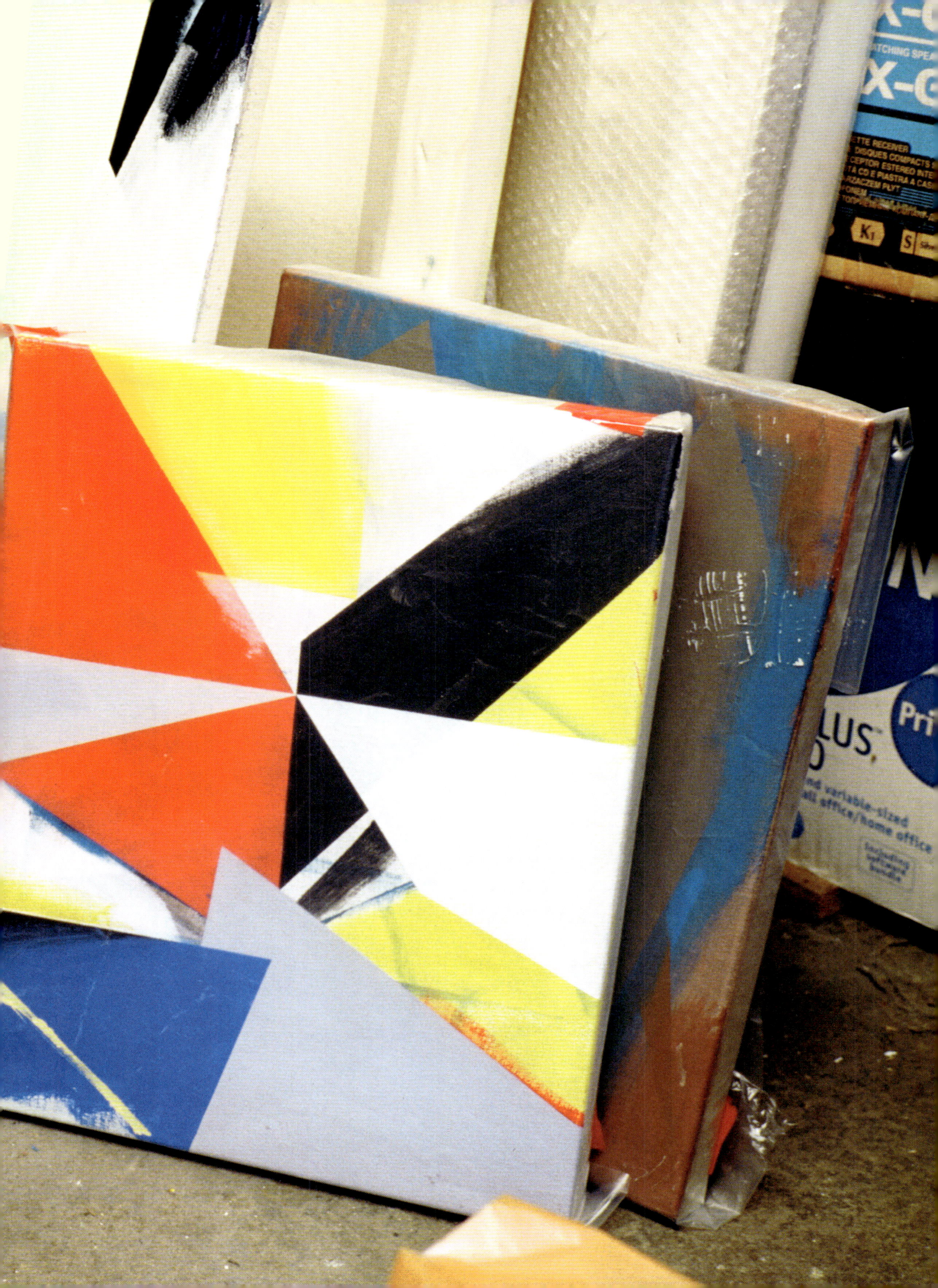

Trump
Francesca Lowe

I once described Francesca Lowe's paintings as being
'like palimpsests, built up layer upon layer through the
constant addition, revision and erasure of material.'[1]
She is a cultural scavenger, culling images and ideas
from sources as varied as fairground signage, an ad
for washing powder or mascara, illustrations for John
Bunyan's book *The Pilgrim's Progress*, Victorian moral
guidance maps or a battle scene in an old master
painting. 'To alleviate the stress of making paintings', she
told me, 'I imagine that I'm simply rubbing off the white
surface of the canvas to reveal the image underneath.
It's as if everything is already there...' Hers for the taking.

For the tapestry, she solved the problem by using
one of her own paintings as source material. Painted
in translucent veils of flesh pink and grey-green, the
painting shows two naked men locked in combat. The
battle appears to be raging on top of the globe or on an
isolated rock, since the figures are silhouetted against
the vast expanse of the heavens.

In preparation for the tapestry, she scanned the image
into a computer and flipped it into the negative, so
reversing the tones and transforming the way the scene
is understood. 'The original painting was very light', says
Lowe, 'and I wanted more contrast; but it has become
more actual and less dreamy – more menacing than
magical.' Surrounded by darkness, the figures now
seem to be in some kind of interior, while the explosive
formations above them appear to be the outcome of
their struggle; if this were a comic strip, the swirls of
vapour would contain words like 'Zap!' and 'Splat!'
but, in this context, they seem more serious and more
sinister. One is tempted to read them as a mushroom
cloud, especially when you discover that Lowe has
added an American rocket to the original painting to
make its bellicose implications more explicit.

The two men – one light, one dark – are represented
only by a tangle of limbs; the lighter figure seems to
be winning, whereas in the painting the situation is

Trump
2.5 x 2m (8ft x 6ft 8in)
Wool and silk tapestry, 2008

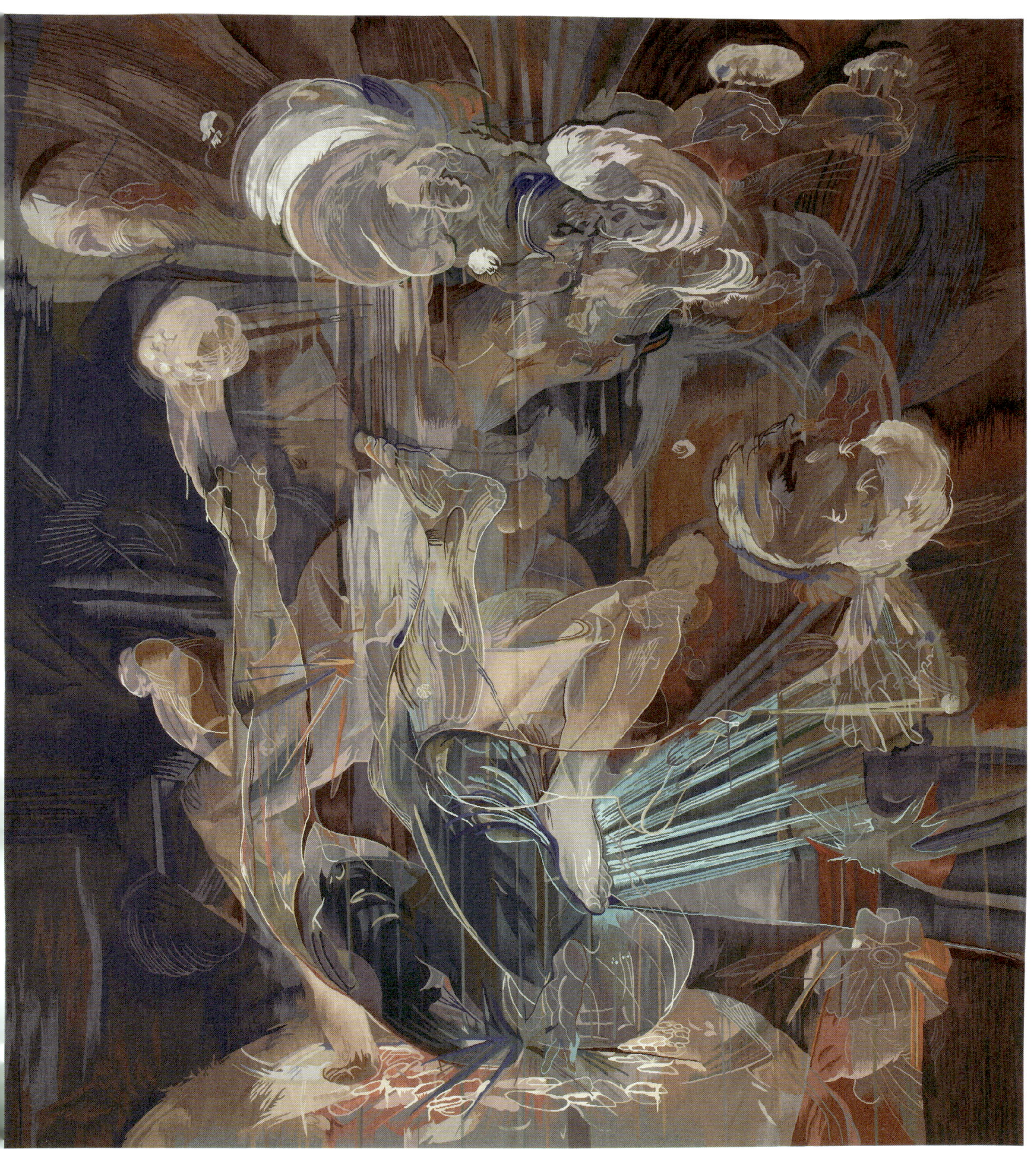

reversed. But, as always in her work, the subject should
not be taken too literally since each image doubles as a
rumination on philosophical issues. Are we witnessing
a mythic struggle, a battle between good and evil? 'It's
not a battle between good and evil, so much as between
two egos', says Lowe. 'The figures represent two states
of being. One is in the ascendence, but the outcome
isn't fixed; things could change. The tapestry is called
'Trump' – as in outranking someone, but also in terms of
sound. I always think of sound in relation to marks; the
soundtrack would be mainly orchestral, along with some
scrapes and phumps.'

Beside the dome on which they are doing battle, stands
a post capped by a cog-shaped wheel, that is seemingly
part of a mechanical device. 'It's short-hand notation for
the mechanics of thought, or being', explains Lowe. 'It's
a metaphor that encourages you to read the rest of the
picture metaphorically.'

The figure on top stamps down hard on his rival,
prompting him to let out an enormous fart of turquoise
gases that fill the air and appear to ignite. 'I was venting
some spleen', says Lowe, 'releasing some gas! It was
an explosion of frustration, a way of reducing tension.
Sometimes you can achieve a lot in a day, but sometimes
nothing changes; time goes slowly and there's frustration
at the monotony of waiting. I don't think the work is
autobiographical, though; it's more about the art historical
source. The figures were probably from a battle scene
by Signorelli.[2] Authorship comes in terms of observation;
that's where the comment lies. And the wider theme is
about the fitting together of things that don't fit and so
create a problem that explodes – metaphorically.'

If this were a scene in an old master painting it would
probably be called 'The Battle of the Titans' and would
have mythic overtones and universal significance. 'That's
just like an old fart!' exclaims Lowe. 'The painting is a
joke about classical mythology and the whole notion of
titanic conflict; but now that the image is dark, it looks

grave rather than humorous; you can't see that it's a
parody on pomposity. The painting is more of a brawl
– a scrap about a scrap – but the tapestry has become
much more serious and old fashioned. It seems to have
returned the image to its source, to have aged and veiled
it so that it becomes difficult to see, like a relic.'

Lowe paints in glazes that reveal the way ideas
accumulate and the imagery grows in visual complexity
and philosophical depth. Transparency is an essential
aspect of her work since it allows ambiguity, the ability
to propose both this and that (opinion, action, outcome)
– to embrace ambivalence. I couldn't imagine an opaque
medium like tapestry capturing this elusive quality and
didn't anticipate a satisfactory translation from the
painted original, so I was astonished by the beauty and
subtlety of her tapestry. Through minute attention to
detail, the weavers have created an almost magical
impression of a translucent, shimmering vision – of
events happening as much on a mental as a physical
plane. 'It has gained an ethereal beauty', Lowe agrees.
'I am blown away by their abilities; it looks amazing.'

[1] Terminus: Francesca Lowe with Alastair Grey, Riflemaker 2007.
[2] Luca Signorelli was an Italian Renaissance artist who specialised in muscular
nudes.

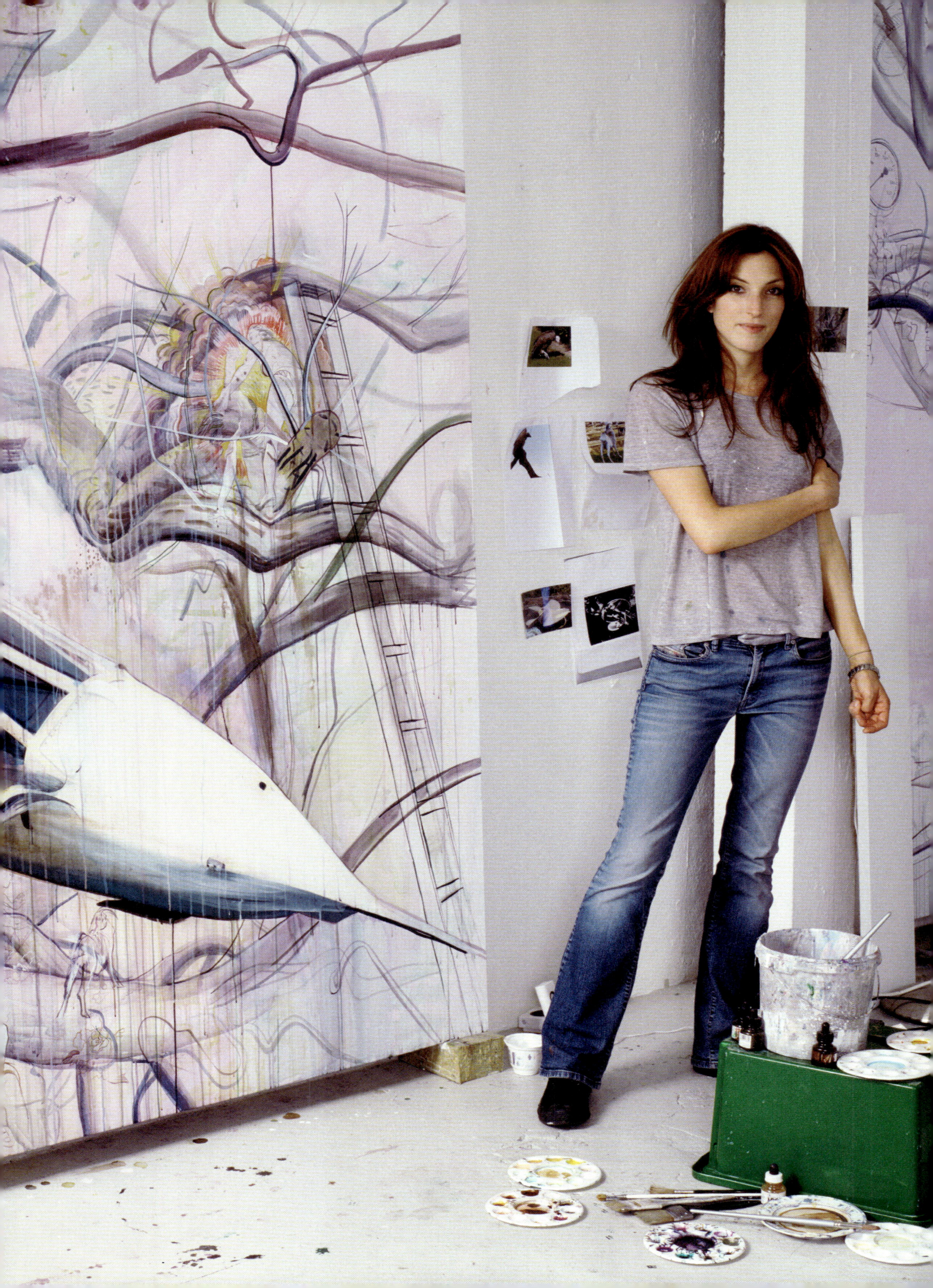

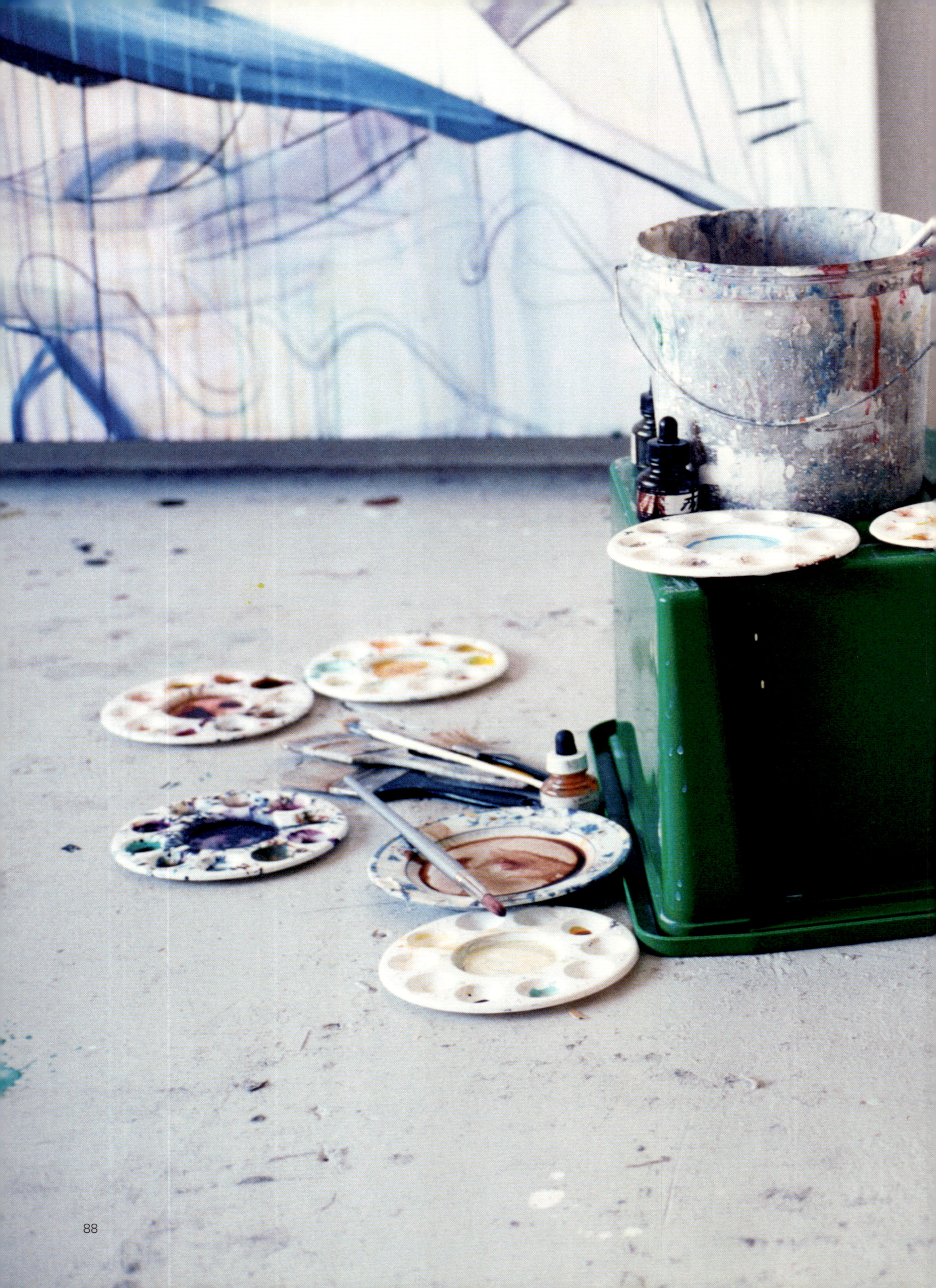

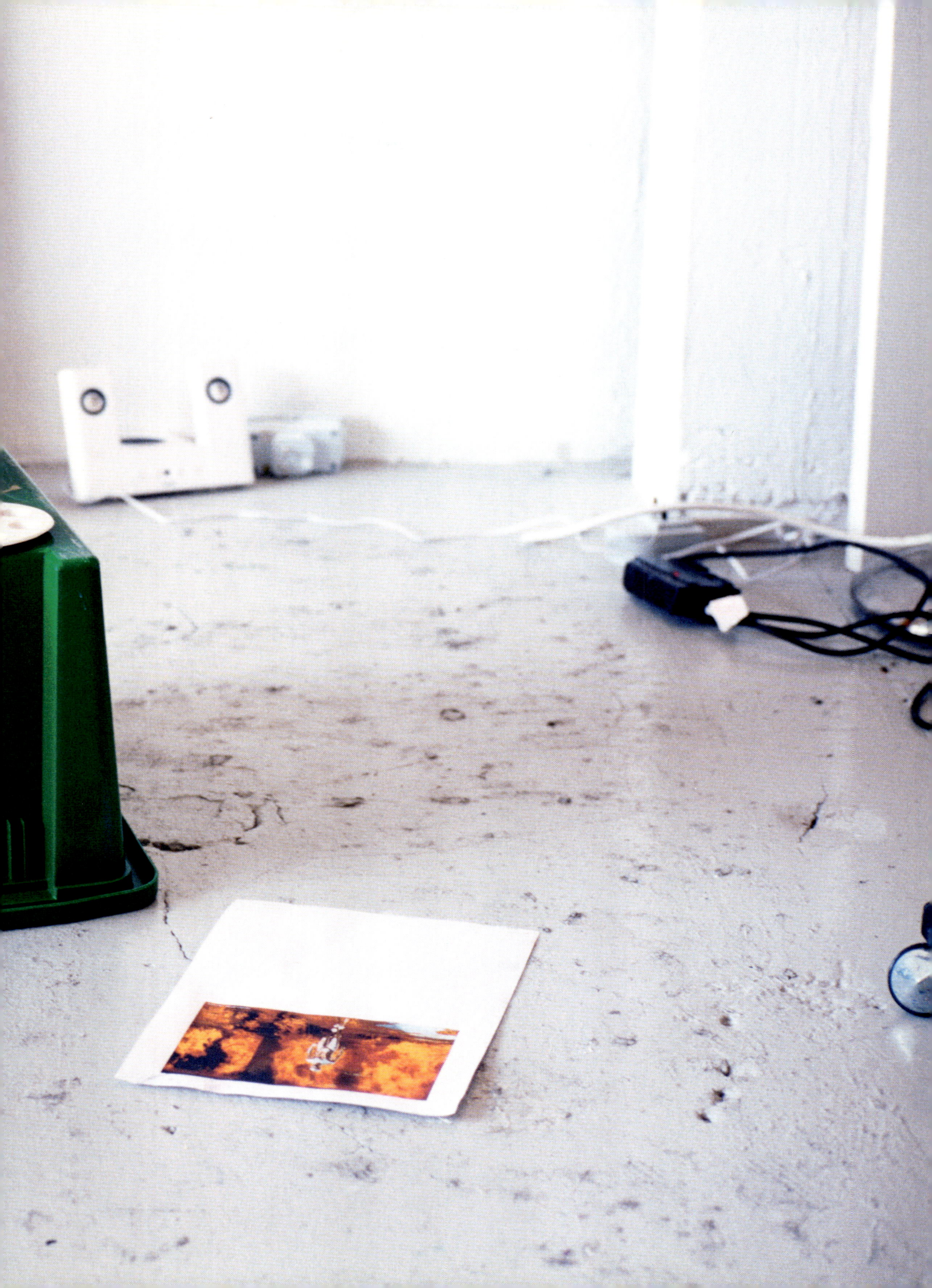

villa joe
Paul Noble

The caption along the bottom of Paul Noble's tapestry
reads: 'Welcome to Nobson's New Personalised Holiday
Villas. Villa Joe Front View'. The image comes from one
of the large, meticulously detailed pencil drawings which
he has been producing since 1995. Using isometric
perspective,[1] Noble has created the fictional city of
Nobson Newtown with its shopping mall, hospital,
cemetery, ruin, chemical plant, slums, palace and villas.

The shape of the buildings is based on letters from
Nobfont, an alphabet specially designed by the artist for
the purpose. So 'villa joe', the modernist structure in the
foreground of the tapestry, spells out its name in sheets
of clear glass three stories high. A utopian exercise in
town-planning that must have gone badly wrong, Nobson
appears to be largely abandoned; most of the buildings
are in a serious state of decay.

'villa joe', on the other hand, is in pristine condition,
perhaps because it is situated outside the city in a
weird landscape resembling a rock-strewn desert. The
building is named after Joe Holtzman, the publisher of
a design magazine called *Nest*, who is obsessed with
ornament and the decorative arts. Through the glass
walls of the museum one can see the exhibits neatly
laid out while, dominating the courtyard, is a sculpture
clearly identifiable as one of the 'turd in the plaza'
forms of public art so derided by American architect,
James Wines.[2] 'I'm not using it as a figure of derision
or disgust', says Noble, 'so much as a symbol of
regeneration, like manure or compost.'

Close inspection reveals that the weird outcrops
surrounding the building are not natural formations
either; the eroded columns and rock piles are based
on actual sculptures. Noble has made an in-depth
study of Henry Moore, 'the first British artist to achieve
international status in the twentieth century.' These
melting monuments look suspiciously like comic strip
versions of the standing and reclining figures to be found
in parks, plazas, courtyards and atriums the world over.

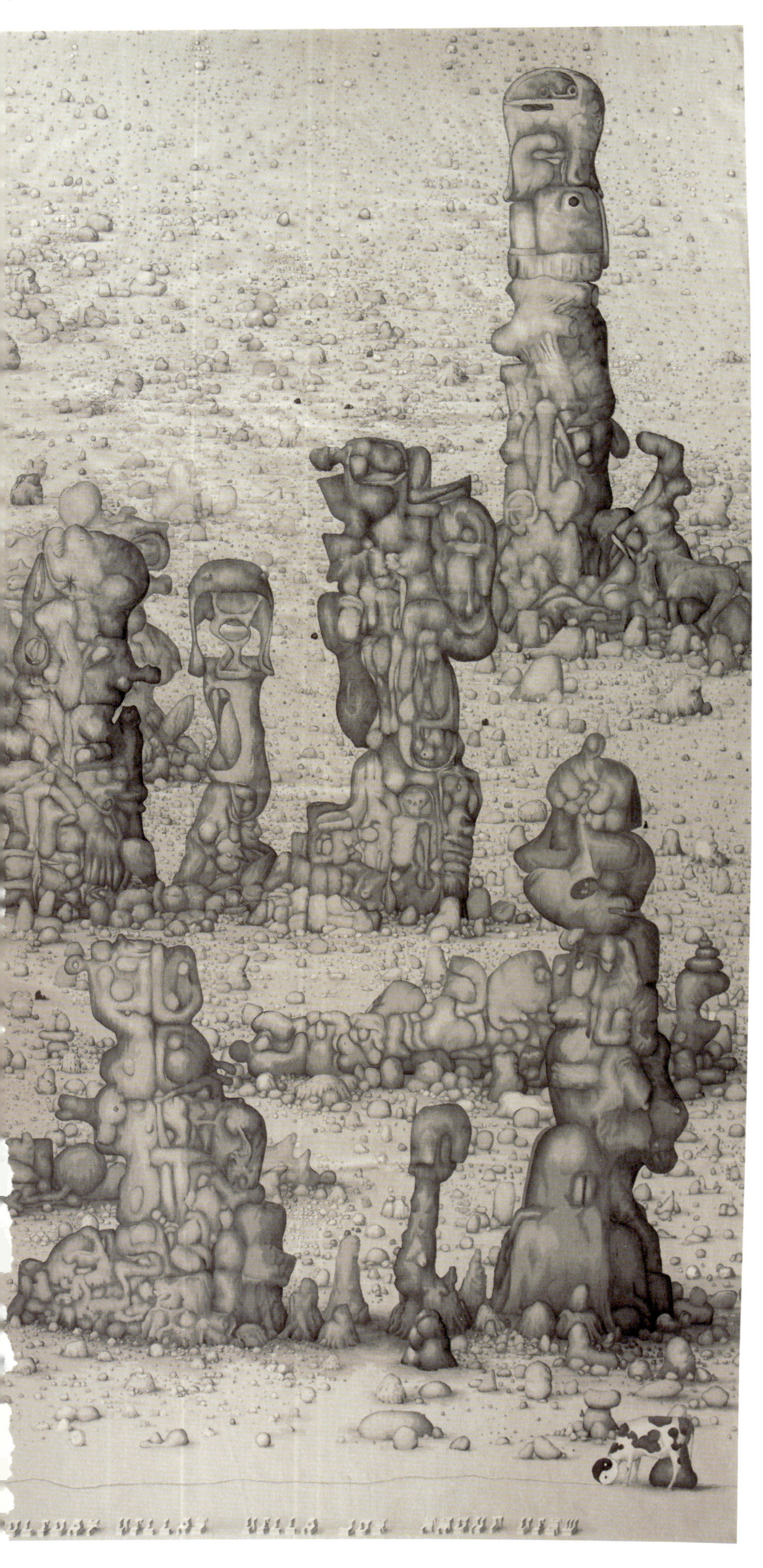

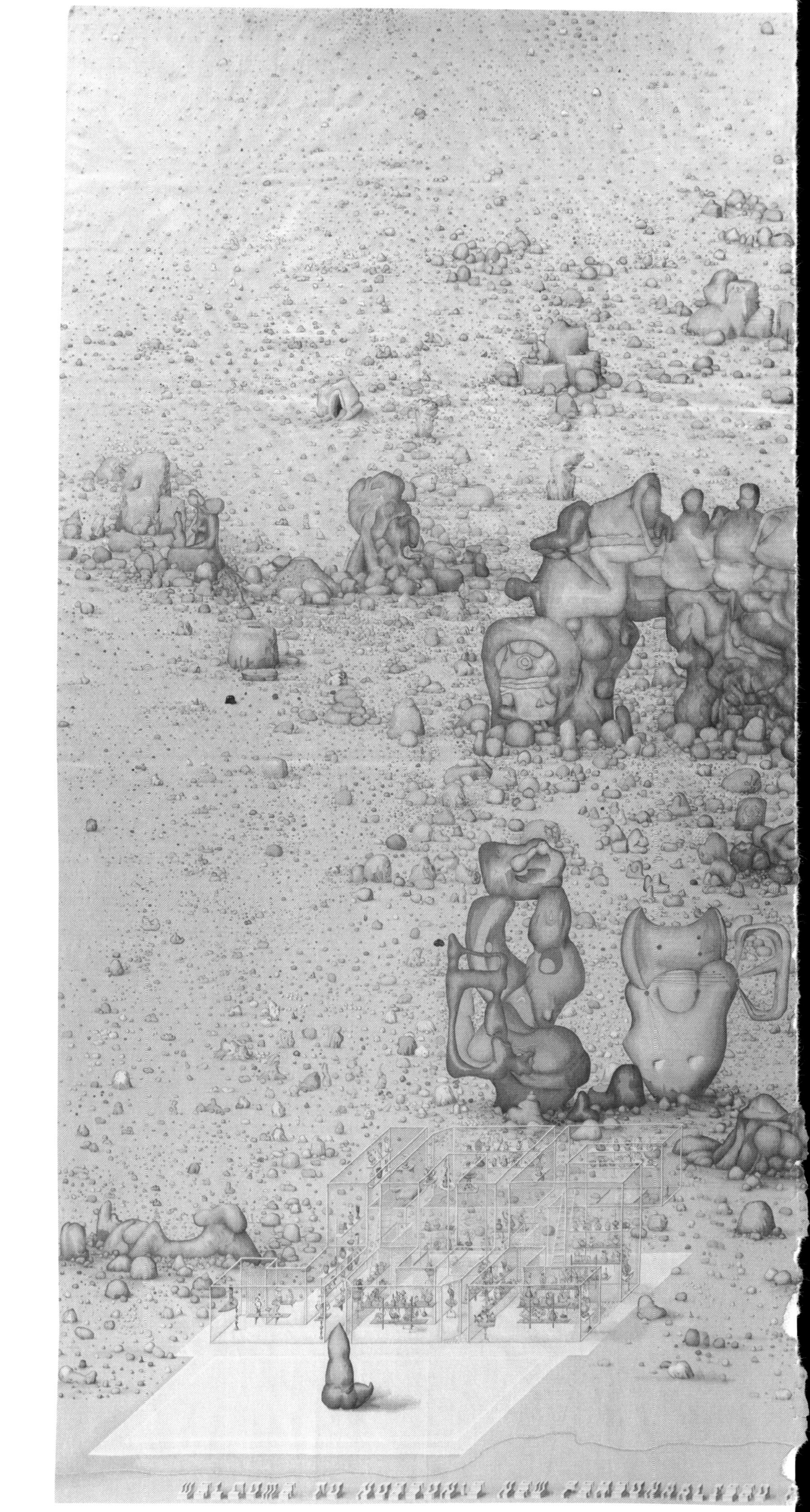

'The mountains around the villa are constructed from neglected Henry Moore sculptures', Noble confirms. It's not the first time he has used the sculptor's work. In his drawing 'Monument Monument' (2007) Moore's sculptures are compressed into a single, craggy monolith. 'At first I was going to draw the sculptures in an orgiastic state', says Noble, 'but I soon began to realise the scale of his achievement, so the drawing changed into a monument to all his monuments.'

Noble chose drawing because he sees it as non-elitist – 'the most commonplace and least problematic art practice'[3] – yet he seems fascinated by artists and architects whose work embodies a utopian vision of society and art's place within it. 'I've always been happy to work within what is known as the low arts. Monumental statements only work in the right context. I'm in Crete at the moment and I'm aware of how earlier civilisations become redundant and how, as time passes, the monumental and the ornamental come together.'

'villa joe' also includes visual puns about the relationship between art and nature. Moore famously liked to go beach-combing in search of flints and pebbles eroded into inspiring shapes and kept a collection of these found treasures in his studio. The stones littering the ground in the tapestry look as if they've tumbled free from the sculptures sprouting in their midst while, conversely, the sculptures could be assemblages of pebbles.

Noble has also made ceramic versions of gongshi or Chinese scholar statues.[4] Rather than basing them on naturally occurring rock formations, though, his are diminutive versions of the organic sculptures made by Moore in response to his beach-combing collection.

Why did he choose this drawing for the tapestry? 'It seems a fitting subject for a tapestry', he says, 'a medium that was once grand, but is now perceived as mainly decorative and belonging to a craft tradition.' For an artist who controls every detail of his intricate

drawings, handing the work over to someone else must have been difficult. He wasn't taking any chances, though. 'I sent a full-sized photograph of the drawing plus a colour print of one section', says Noble, 'since I use tone like colour. I work with very hard, 8H pencils and you can only achieve a certain degree of darkness, so they are used like watercolour – I build up the tone with shading, then rub it back with soft paper to get a glaze. The tapestry is twice the size of the drawing, so it's incredibly detailed and the weavers had to make an outline copy of all the shapes, annotated with all the colours. I feel enormous sympathy for them!'

[1] In isometric perspective, receding lines remain parallel; it is often employed by architects for its clarity, since it gives a bird's eye view without the distortions produced by recession.
[2] In the 1960s, Wines coined the term *Plop* art to refer to large, abstract sculptures made for public spaces but thoughtlessly 'plopped' in position, without taking account of the audience or the surroundings.
[3] Quoted by Katharine Stout in *Days Like These*, Tate 2003.
[4] For centuries, scholars in China have collected rocks eroded into exotic shapes and placed them on pedestals as though they were sculptures. They are known as gongshi.

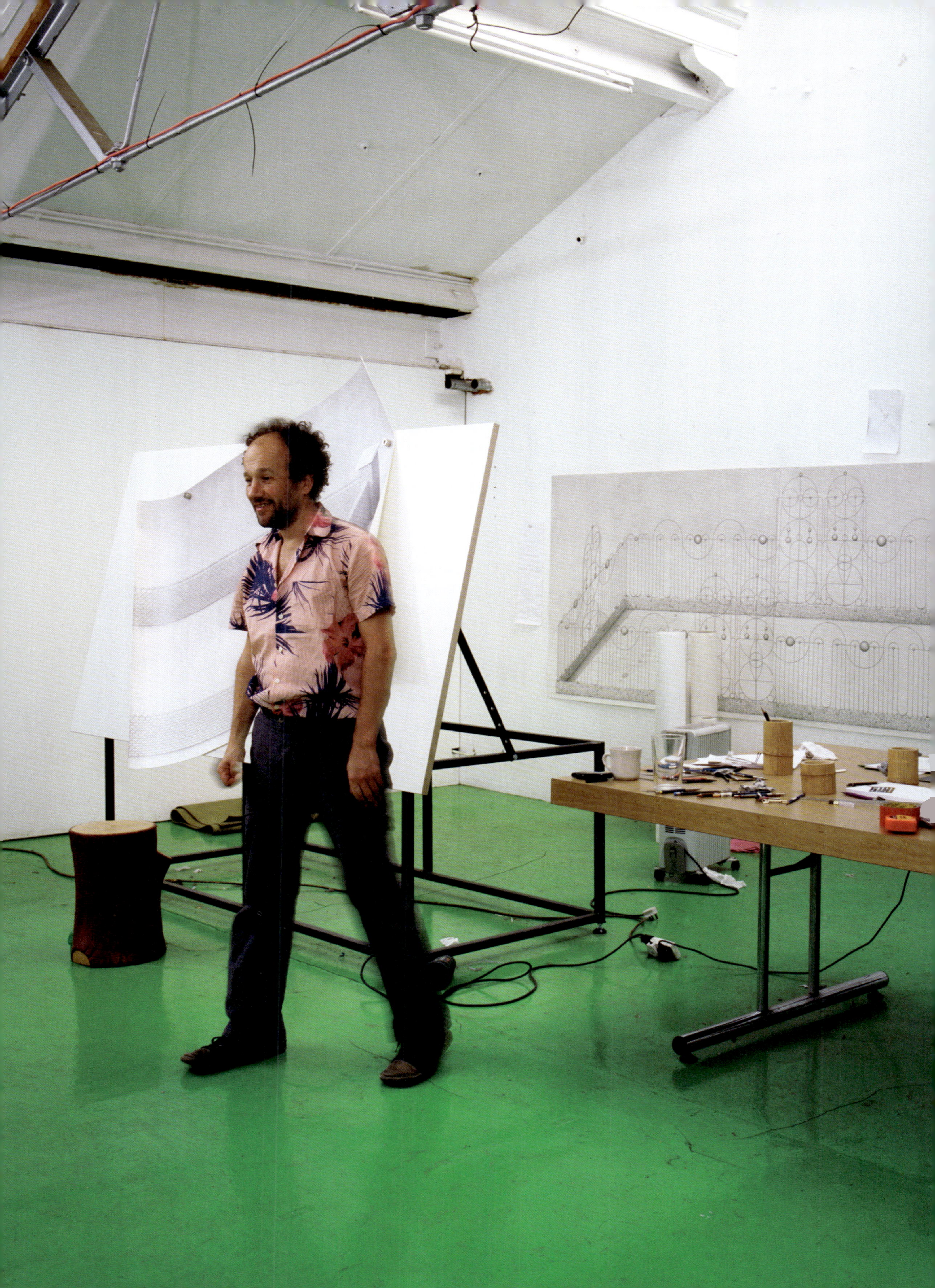

Pathology of Suspension
Shahzia Sikander

During a residency at the Fabric Workshop and Museum
in Philadelphia, in 2006, Shahzia Sikander produced 'The
Illustrated Page'. A combination of silkscreen, gold leaf
and gouache paint, it takes the form of an open book.
To show how the design was put together, the layers
that make up these exquisite pages are reproduced in
the catalogue of her exhibition at the Irish Museum of
Modern Art in Dublin.

Her tapestry is the shape of the left-hand page, and
contains many of the same elements. The first layer
consists of a decorative border in yellow on black,
resembling a floral repeat pattern by William Morris,
and a rectangle of plain red which frames a simplified
landscape. In the tapestry, the space between the border
and frame is filled with botanical illustrations of flowers
among which butterflies flit and birds sing. To my eye,
these elements look Victorian but, explains Sikander,
they were inspired by Indian and Persian miniatures
from the Moghul period, a tradition in which she trained
in the late 1980s, at the National Art School in Lahore.
'Over the centuries, a lot of influences went back and
forth between Europe and Asia', she tells me, 'through
the East India Company, for instance; and a lot of the
borders were influenced by Dutch prints. I observe
these relationships, but I don't approach things in an art
historical manner.'

She left Pakistan in 1993 to study in the United States,
where she now lives. In her work she sets up a complex
dialogue between past and present, East and West,
abstraction and figuration. Images are superimposed
in successive layers that disregard, contradict, veil
or complement one another and, in the tapestry, this
interplay is unusually clear.

Taken from the right hand page of 'The Illustrated Page',
the central landscape seems to belong to a different era
from the borders. In 2003 Sikander made a series of
paintings called 'Land Escapes' inspired by the deserts
of Southern California, which she has photographed

Pathology of Suspension
2.7 x 1.86m (8ft 10in x 6ft 1in)
Wool and silk tapestry with raised silk embroidery, 2008

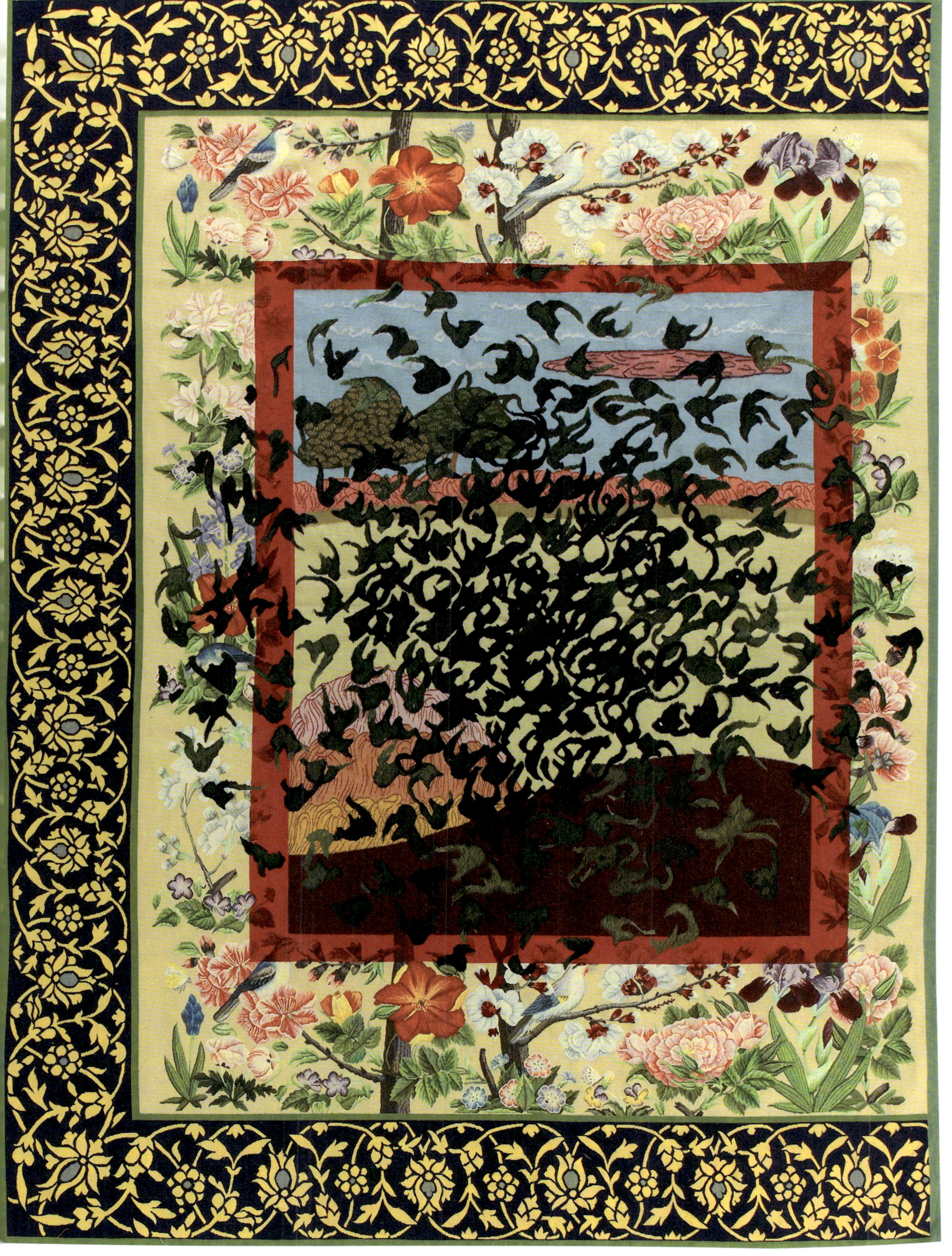

repeatedly. 'The intense colours of the desert were a constant reminder of the saturated colour palettes of Rajasthani/Rajput painting', she has said. 'I was seeking in my mind a relationship between the old paintings and my immediate environment, (and) the light and its subliminal beauty in the surrounding desert scapes became the link.'[1]

She also studied the Indian miniatures in the San Diego Museum of Art and both influences are apparent in the 'Land Escapes', where space has been flattened and the landscape simplified to a few basic elements. In the tapestry, a pink cloud hangs above two lollipop trees growing on the horizon. Between them and the hill in the foreground is an expanse of yellow ochre interrupted only by three hillocks. It's as though the figures had been removed from an Indian miniature to leave open ground – except that the handling is contemporary; the elements would not look amiss in a painting by David Hockney.

The landscape is obscured by a swarm of dark shapes that also appears in 'The Illustrated Page'; they originate in a video titled 'SpiNN', from 2003, which features a traditional Mughal durbar hall populated by gopi women, devotées of the Hindu God Krishna. Suddenly their stylised black hairdos assume a life of their own to gather in a dense cluster over the heads of the remaining women and obliterate them. In the tapestry, the unruly flock escapes from the landscape to flap about like spirits released from bondage. 'I have a bank of images with which I take a lot of artistic freedom', says Sikander, 'including bodily and cultural removal from their origins.'

Mastering the art of the miniature requires prolonged application and careful study of the tradition; contemporary artists, on the other hand, are expected to establish independent voices. It is tempting to see the clash between confining borders and the unruly elements escaping them as a metaphor for the balance that Sikander seeks between her rigorous training and her desire to relate to daily life. 'I've used hair and unruly

geometric structures in multiple ways', she confirms. 'It's almost like a form of portraiture, elaborating the desire to translate images from one situation and location to another.'

What made her decide to do the tapestry? 'I have a compulsion to draw', she says, 'but I'm taking it in as many directions as possible; the context creates the meaning of an image. On a large scale like the tapestry, the image doesn't retain its detail; it becomes less delicate and more confrontational.'

Did handing her design over to a third party cause concern? 'I have a lot of assistants working for me in the studio', says Sikander, 'and also doing wall drawings, so handing over my designs was no problem. I scanned the drawing into a computer and enlarged it to the actual size; then it was vectorised to remove the pixels, so the weavers had an exact reference point. They've used different kinds of weaving – some very fine, some less so; the cluster of hair, for instance, is thicker and sits on top in relief. It's all done in silk and has been very beautifully handled.'

[1] Quoted by Rachel Kent in 'Intimate Immensity' Museum of Contemporary Art, Sydney 2007.

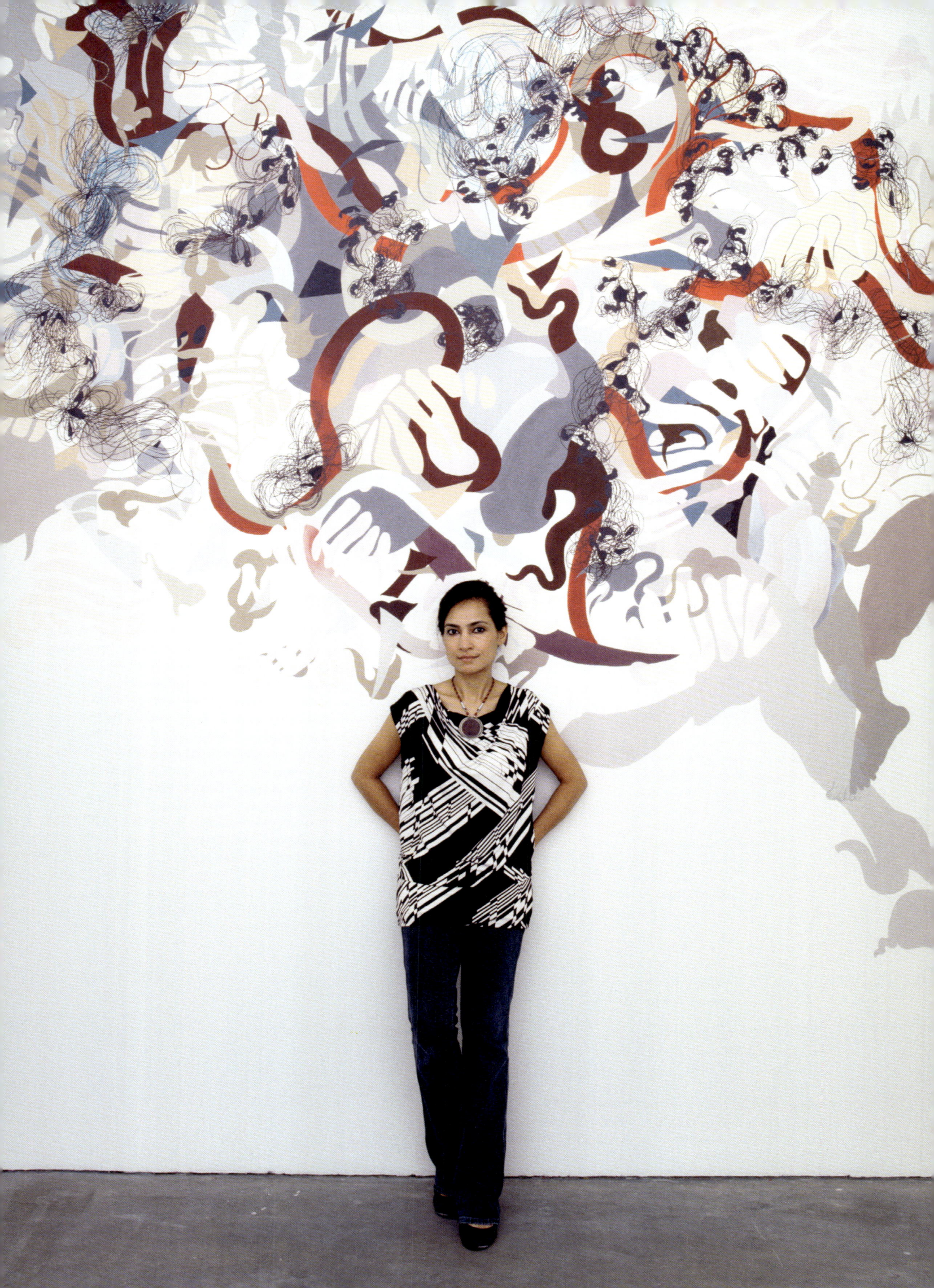

Alphabet
Peter Blake

Before going to the Royal College of Art in 1953, Peter Blake spent a year studying graphic design, because he'd been told it gave him more chance of earning a living. He had already studied typography and lettering along with drawing, silversmithing and joinery at Gravesend Technical College (where he was a student from the age of 14) and his fascination for all things typographic was cemented during that year. 'I can actually set up type and letterpress and do that kind of thing,' he told Mel Gooding.[1] 'My craft option for the Intermediate was Roman Lettering, so I was actually taught how to make a letter form, the seraphs and the spacing, and that's something that stays with you for ever.'

He even applied for the graphic design department at the Royal College, but also submitted a painting and was accepted in fine art. Despite being the godfather of British Pop Art, he is still best known for the cover he designed for the Beatles album *Sgt. Pepper's Lonely Hearts Club Band* in 1967 – more than 40 years ago. The brightly coloured crowd of people was collaged together using cut-outs that include screen idols such as Charlie Chaplin and Marylin Monroe. Wearing psychedelic uniforms the Beatles stand in the middle, above a drum bearing the name of the album and a garden planted in red flowers with the name of the band.

The painted drum and flowers spell out a message, but they are also pictures in their own right. And this duality is what most seems to fascinate Blake, the design student who became a painter only to return to design again and again. 'The paintings I make', he has said, 'are often simply about... presenting a particular type, and I use commercial design devices, lettering and division and so on. Maybe it's a cross I have to bear, this graphic design training.'[1]

Curiously enough, books did not feature much in his childhood. He was evacuated the day after war was declared and, from the age of seven until 14, was mostly separated from his parents. 'It was a difficult time to be a

Alphabet
1.8 x 1.8m (5ft 11in x 5ft 11in)
Wool, silk and artificial silk tapestry, 2008

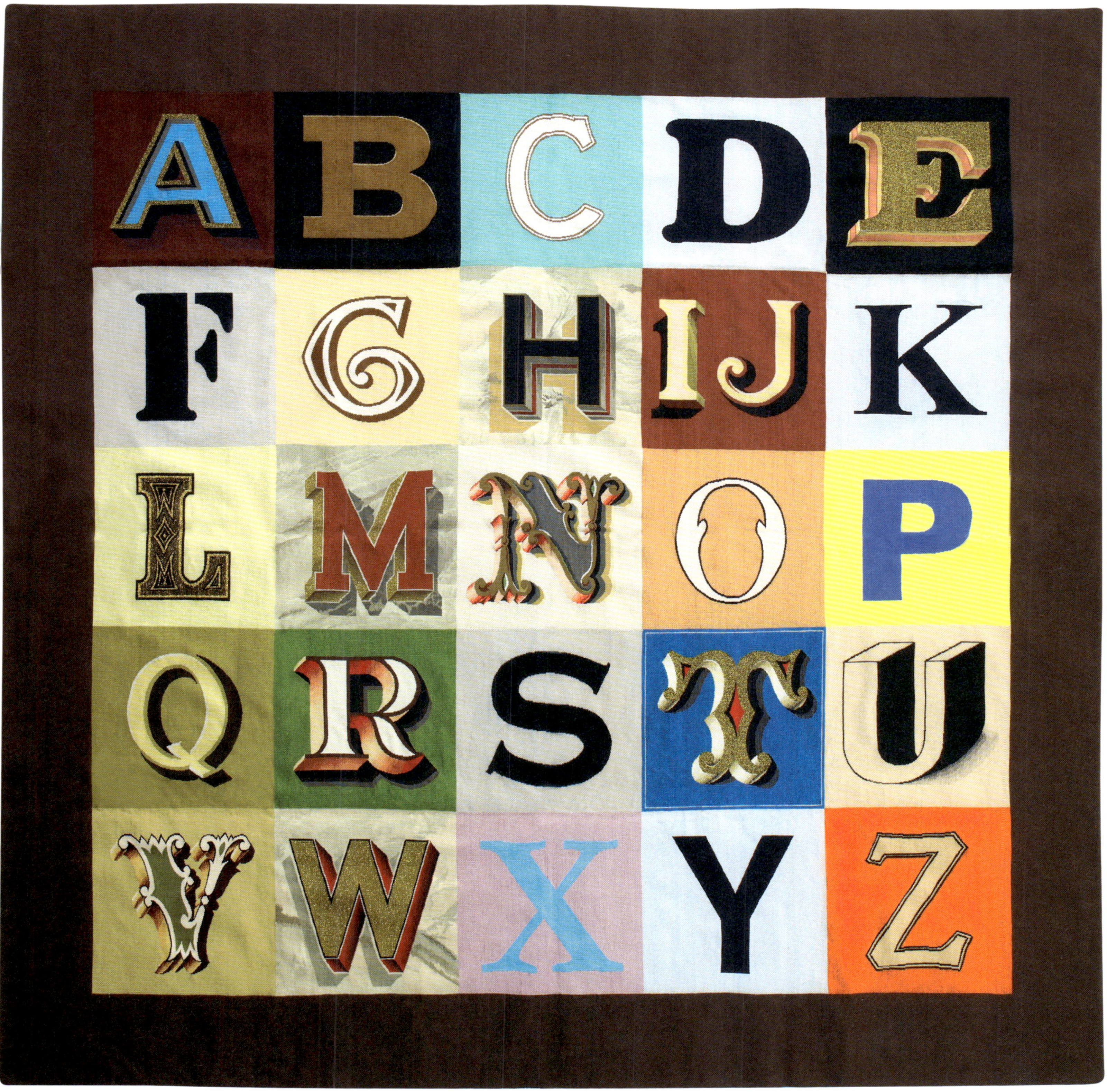
A B C D E
F G H I J K
L M N O P
Q R S T U
V W X Y Z

child', he recalls, 'particularly not to be with your parents. In a way I might be compensating for that and always going back... the work is often about childhood.'[1] It often harks back, I would suggest, to the period in childhood before one can read fluently, when letters appear exotic but indecipherable, and one experiences them primarily as images.

He is an avid collector of ephemera and, over the years, has amassed a huge assortment of letter forms and the imagery associated with them. As you can tell from the tapestry, he loves exotic letters that encourage one to ponder the context in which they might have been used – whether on a fairground ride, circus caravan or steam train; a Wanted poster, billboard or handbill; a shop front, or stamped on the side of a crate.

And over the years, Blake has made many prints featuring alphabets. His 'Alphabet' of 1991 works like an 'A is for apple' children's book with 'M' for Marilyn Monroe and 'K' for Elvis Presley – the King. Alongside these all time greats are some less obvious choices such as 'Ornithology' for 'O' and a collage of 'Unusual People' for 'U'. Recently he has produced a beautiful set of silkscreen prints each illustrating a different letter in words and pictures, including semaphore signs, hand signals and Morse code as well as the letter form.

What made him want to embark on the tapestry? 'I've always been interested in craft, and I've been working on rugs and jewelry', he explains, 'so the tapestry project was an interesting way to work in yet another medium. I had already been working on a number of alphabets and the tapestry was a further variation. Some of the letters are quite exotic because I knew they could be translated well into fabric and thread.'

Some letters are completely flat, but others look as if they are in relief. Were there any surprises in the way they translated into woven thread? 'The proofing stage – that time between handing over a design to the craftsmen, who then send back a finished proof to scale – was very exciting', he recalls. 'Seeing the gold thread was also very exciting; the difference between looking at the 'Alphabet' on screen and seeing it in real life was when dull gold suddenly becomes gold thread.'

Prints can hang almost anywhere, but is there somewhere that he thinks would be especially appropriate for the tapestry? 'I would love to see the tapestry in the British Library', he says. 'The art budget there was slashed and all commissions were cancelled, so the Kitaj tapestry had to be privately funded. It would be fitting to hang an 'Alphabet' in there.'

[1] Interviewed by Mel Gooding in *An Alphabet* by Peter Blake, Coriander Studio and Paul Stolper Gallery, 2007.

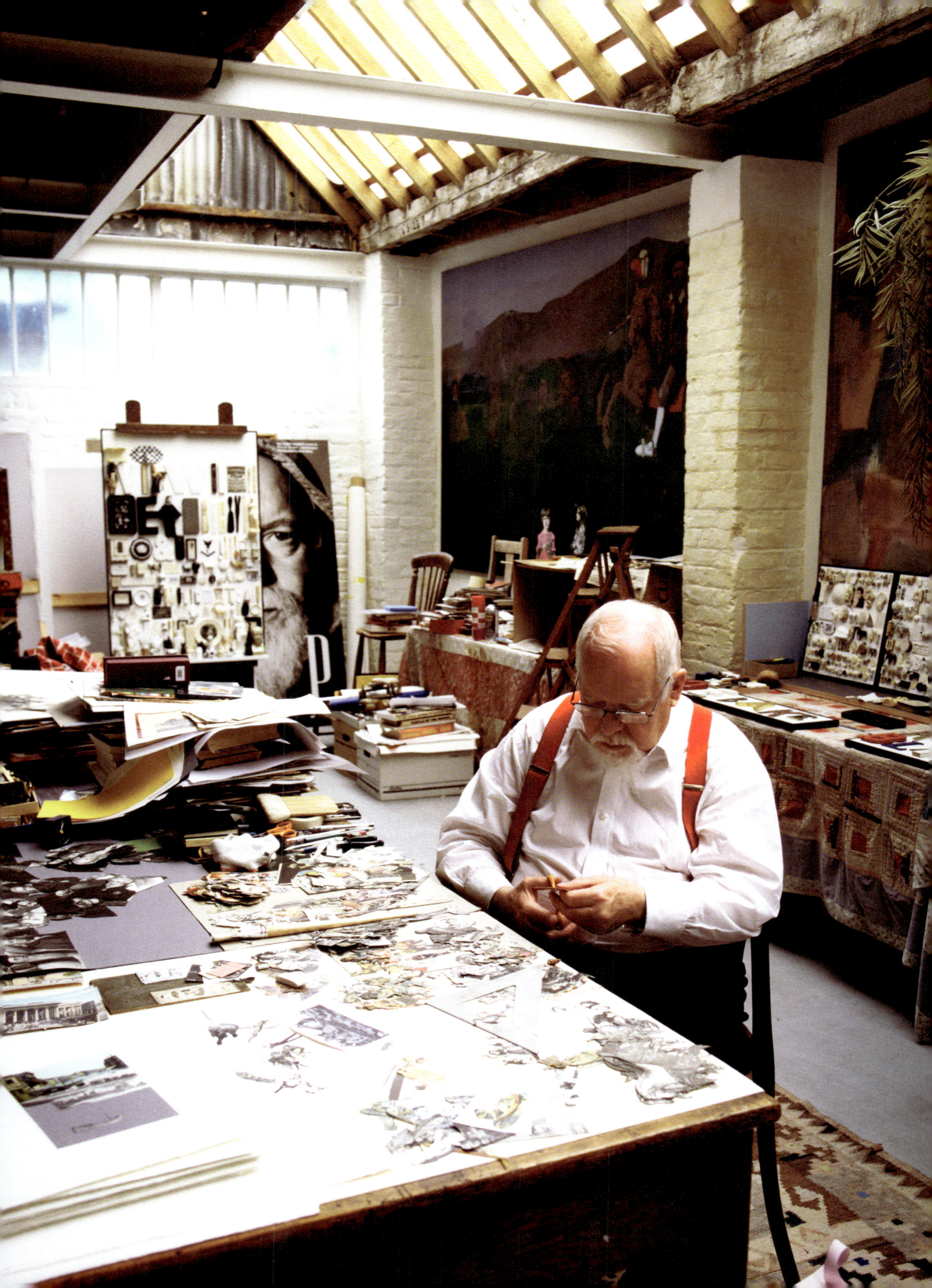

DAMIANI

Damiani editore
via Zanardi, 376
40131 Bologna
t. +39 051 63 50 805
f. +39 051 63 47 188
info@damianieditore.it
www.damianieditore.com

ISBN 978-88-6208-076-7

Printed in September 2008
by Grafiche Damiani, Bologna.

BANNERS OF PERSUASION
119B Portland Road
London
W11 4LN

T +44 (0)20 7243 7345
E sophie@bannersofpersuasion.com
W www.bannersofpersuasion.com

Published on occasion of the exhibition

'Demons, Yarns & Tales'

The Dairy
7 Wakefield Street
London
WC1 1PG
United Kingdom

10–22 November 2008

The Loft
NE 1st Court
Miami
Florida 33137
United States

3–6 December 2008

Photography by Dan Stevens
Production photography by Andrew Rowat
Beatriz Milhazes' portrait by João Wainer

With thanks to:
Tot Taylor, Virginia Damsta, Paul Stolper, Julian Balme,
Mark Fletcher, Dan Stevens and the artists' galleries.

Use of images of works courtesy of the following:

avaf is represented by Peres Projects, Berlin & Los
Angeles

Beatriz Milhazes is represented by Stephen Friedman
Gallery, London

Francesca Lowe is represented by Riflemaker, London

Fred Tomaselli is represented by White Cube, London

Gary Hume is represented by White Cube, London

Gavin Turk is represented by Riflemaker, London

Ghada Amer & Reza Farkhondeh are represented
by Gagosian Gallery, New York

Grayson Perry is represented by Victoria Miro, London

Jaime Gili is represented by Riflemaker, London

Julie Verhoeven is represented by Riflemaker, London

Kara Walker is represented by Sikkema Jenkins & Co.,
New York

Peter Blake is represented by Waddington Galleries,
London

Paul Noble is represented by Maureen Paley, London

Shahzia Sikander is represented by Sikkema Jenkins
& Co., New York

Some of the tapestry images in this book are renderings
made up from the artists' original artwork rather than
photographs of the finished tapestries*. This is because
three of the final works were not finished in time for
the book's publication. Some of the images in this book
will therefore vary slightly to the final tapestry works
exhibited in the show 'Demons, Yarns & Tales'.
*avaf, Gavin Turk, and Kara Walker

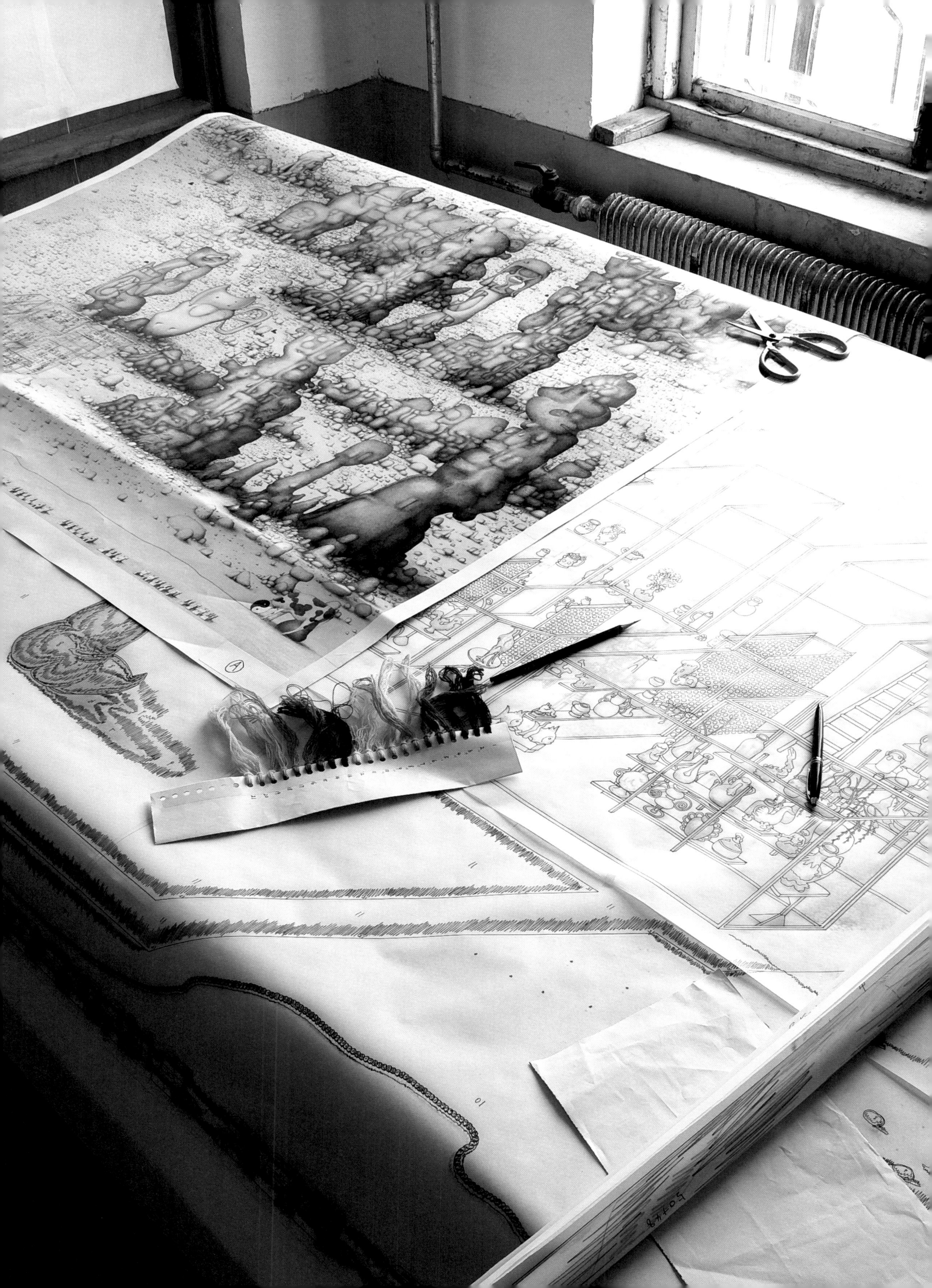

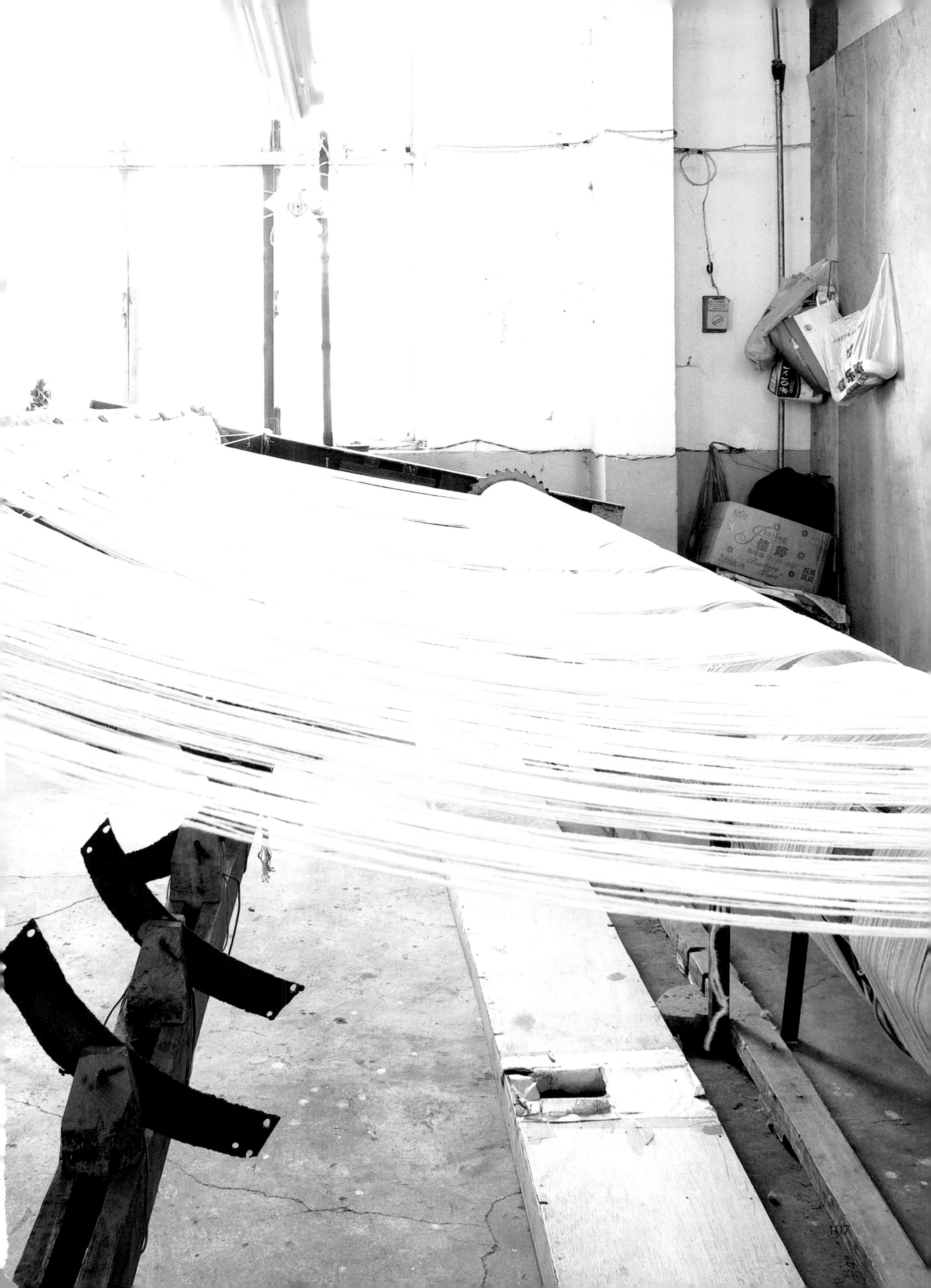